LIVING YOUR OWN LIFE
Existential Analysis in Action

Edited by
Silvia Längle and Christopher Wurm

KARNAC

First published in 2016 by
Karnac Books Ltd
118 Finchley Road
London NW3 5HT

British Library Cataloguing in Publication Data

A C.I.P. for this book is available from the British Library

ISBN-13: 978-1-78220-360-5

Typeset by V Publishing Solutions Pvt Ltd., Chennai, India

Printed in Great Britain by TJ International Ltd, Padstow, Cornwall

www.karnacbooks.com

CONTENTS

ABOUT THE EDITORS AND CONTRIBUTORS

All authors in this collection are psychotherapists belonging to the Gesellschaft für Logotherapie und Existenzanalyse (GLE)—Society for Logotherapy and Existential Analysis, Vienna.

Rupert Dinhobl, Mag.theol. Dr. theol.

Born 1955 in Vienna. Psychotherapist on the Crisis Intervention Ward of the Christian-Doppler-Klinik of the University of Salzburg and in private practice, teaching supervisor of the Society for Logotherapy and Existential Analysis.

Helene Drexler, Dr. phil.

Born 1961. Clinical and health psychologist, existential analyst in private practice, supervisor and training therapist of the Austrian Society for Logotherapy and Existential Analysis, lecturer at the University of Vienna.

Astrid Görtz, Mag. Dr. phil.

Clinical and health psychologist, existential analyst in private practice, supervisor and training therapist of the Austrian Society for Logotherapy and Existential Analysis, lecturer at the University of Vienna and the Sigmund Freud Private University in Vienna, acting editor-in-chief of the journal *EXISTENZANALYSE*.

Christoph Kolbe, Dr. paed.

Born 1955. Psychological psychotherapist; Diploma in Education; doctoral studies in psychology, pedagogy, theology; active in private practice; founder of the North German Institute for Existential Analysis and Logotherapy, co-director of the Academy for Existential Analysis and Logotherapy (with S. Jaeger-Gerlach), lecturer at the Universities of Vienna and Hannover, diverse publications and international lectures, Chairman of the German Society for Logotherapy and Existential Analysis.

Alfried Längle, Dr. med. Dr. phil. Univ. Professor

Born 1951. Studied medicine and psychology in Innsbruck, Rome, Toulouse, and Vienna. General medical practitioner and psychotherapist; clinical psychologist; teaching supervisor of the Society for Logotherapy and Existential Analysis; professor at HSE University Moscow; guest professor at Sigmund Freud University in Vienna and senior academic assistant (*Privatdozent*) at the University of Klagenfurt; President of the International Society for Logotherapy and Existential Analysis; and active in psychotherapy practice.

Silvia Längle, Dr. phil.

Psychotherapist, training therapist of the Austrian Society for Logotherapy and Existential Analysis, board member of the International Society for Logotherapy and Existential Analysis, and editor-in-chief of the journal *EXISTENZANALYSE*.

Anton Nindl, Mag. Dr. phil.

Born 1956. Clinical and health psychologist, pedagogue, psychotherapist in private practice, training therapist of the Austrian Society for

Logotherapy and Existential Analysis, Director of the Institute for Existential Analysis in Salzburg.

Christian Probst, Dr. med.

Specialist in psychiatry and neurology, psychotherapist, training therapist of the Austrian Society for Logotherapy and Existential Analysis, board member of the International Society for Logotherapy and Existential Analysis, Director of the Institute for Existential Analysis in Graz.

Michaela Probst (deceased)

Pedagogue and existential analyst in private practice, training therapist of the Austrian Society for Logotherapy and Existential Analysis, board member of the Austrian Society for Logotherapy and Existential Analysis, Co-director of the Institute for Existential Analysis and Logotherapy in Graz.

Karl Rühl, Deacon

Born 1962. Managing director, existential analyst.

Karin Steinert, Mag. phil.

Psychologist and existential analyst in private practice, training therapist of the Austrian Society for Logotherapy and Existential Analysis, lecturer at the University of Vienna, editor of the journal EXISTENZANALYSE.

Liselotte Tutsch, Dr. phil.

Clinical and health psychologist, existential analyst, supervisor, coach, training therapist, trauma therapist.

Christine Wicki, Dipl. theol.

Born 1956. Studied theology and philosophy. Psychotherapist, supervisor, and training therapist of the Swiss Society for Logotherapy and Existential Analysis.

Christopher Simon Essery Wurm, MB BS FRACGP FAChAM

Born 1956. Studied medicine at the University of Adelaide, trained in Logotherapy and Existential Analysis in Vienna, gained experience as a psychotherapist in Austria (1991). Senior consultant, Drug and Alcohol Resource Unit, Royal Adelaide Hospital, and Sefton Park Primary Health Care Services; GP psychotherapist in private practice; Visiting Fellow, Discipline of Psychiatry, University of Adelaide.

FOREWORD

Christopher Wurm

This book aims to highlight new applications and methods in the practice of existential analysis. Viktor Frankl's logotherapy has become internationally recognised through books, journal articles, and audio-visual recordings in several languages, but this is the first book in English to outline the ways in which the approach has developed, mainly in Vienna, during the last twenty-five years.

Until now, there has been almost no literature available in English on the current application of existential analysis. We chose this book (first edited by Silvia Längle and Martha Sulz in Austria) because the majority of papers deal more with the *application* of existential analysis than the theory. We hope this makes the approach more accessible and understandable to practitioners—and to a broader public interested in the themes of psychotherapy, counselling, and existence.

My way

How did I get involved with existential analysis, growing up in a household in South Australia where only English was spoken? My family members who might have once spoken German probably had to be careful to speak only English from about 1914, with one ancestor changing his name from Wurm to Weston. While South Australia did have a considerable number of settlers from various German-speaking kingdoms, dukedoms, duchies, and principalities, who arrived within the first twenty years of it being founded as a British colony, any suspicion of allegiance to the "old country" could lead to internment (notwithstanding that Westphalia, Bavaria, Prussia, etc. had ceased to exist and the British Royal Family also had many ancestors from that part of Europe!).

But one night when I was at home feeling uninspired by the pictures of muscle and liver tissue in my pathology textbook, I became captivated by a television programme my parents were watching. There was a man with a continental accent talking about psychotherapy in a way that completely challenged my prejudices. He said, "Some people are unhappy, not because of their past, but because of the way they deal with the present." The programme was an Australian Broadcasting Commission interview with Viktor Frankl. From that day forward, I listened intently to everything I could about psychotherapy at university, but not once did I hear a word about existentialism, meaning, or purpose.

I qualified as a medical practitioner, but opted not to take up the offer of training in psychiatry, as I felt that might be at odds with my interest in existential analysis. A specialist discipline in "addiction medicine" was later created. On the basis of my involvement in undergraduate and postgraduate teaching, including book chapters and conference presentations outlining applications of existential analysis to the field, I was made a "Foundation Fellow of the Australasian Chapter of Addiction Medicine".

Cultural differences

I spent two months as a medical student on an elective at the University of Bonn. I was looking forward to an opportunity to travel and to become better acquainted with the German language and culture. I also planned to meet up with Australian classmates and old family friends in England and Scotland over Christmas and Hogmanay.

I had often found that social interactions in my English-speaking circles tended to value maintaining harmonious conversation, and avoiding conflict. There was a convention that it was best not to discuss sex, politics, or religion. In Bonn, I found that my new acquaintances were much more likely to speak passionately about issues that they cared deeply about. Indeed, I soon found myself in conversations about nuclear power, renewable energy, peace, and the meaning of Lou Reed's song lyrics. More than thirty years later, in spite of searching, it still seems harder to find someone willing to have these conversations in English.

I had the impression that the concepts and words for meaning and purpose are sought after universally, but that they are spoken of more willingly and with greater fluency (and less self-consciousness) in continental Europe than the English-speaking world. Or was my hometown of Adelaide not representative of other English-speaking communities?

Why did it take so long for interest in existential analysis to develop in Australia, North America, and the UK? There is unlikely to be any greater need to explore meaning and purpose between cultures, but there may be either a different level of willingness—or a better familiarity with the concepts. Just as French was once thought of as the language of poets and novelists, German has been prominent as the language of twentieth-century philosophers.

Surely English-speakers don't have any less need for poetry or philosophy in the basic sense of reflecting on one's own existence. Perhaps some of us are reluctant to explore these topics because it's harder to find the words to express the concepts—or because it's riskier to talk about values and dilemmas than sport or the weather.

As attitudes and interests change, I believe that the uptake of this book could show that the English-speaking world is very open to exploring philosophical issues and using existential analysis to deal with life's challenges.

Sometimes individuals act aggressively because they have been brought up to hold back from expressing emotions such as sadness or anxiety. People may also express distress when they struggle with difficult situations, such as a loss or competing sets of values. Without clients and clinicians alike understanding key existential questions, there is an increasing risk that their distress will be mistakenly thought to be a form of illness, when it is more appropriate to view it as an understandable response to their dilemma.

Existential analysis and logotherapy

Until the early 1980s logotherapy was only available through Frankl's lectures and books. To improve this situation, Frankl's long-standing assistant, the psychiatrist Eva Kozdera, the psychologist Gabriele

Vesely (Frankl's daughter), and the physician and psychologist Alfried Längle established "Training in Existential Analysis and Logotherapy" in Vienna in 1982.

For a young Australian keen to learn, this was perfect timing. I enrolled in the course in the second half of 1984 and made trips back to Vienna several times. I spent a three-month period working in a hospital in Feldkirch, Western Austria in 1991 and was invited to speak at a conference in Graz organized by the Gesellschaft für Logotherapie und Existenzanalyse (GLE). My paper was published as a chapter in the proceedings, edited by Alfried Längle and Christian Probst (Wurm, 1991).

As well as his own methods, Längle introduced self-experience into the training. Viktor Frankl decided to resign from his position as honorary president of the Society of Logotherapy and Existential Analysis in 1991, mainly because of the use of self-experience in the training. Frankl considered the use of self-experience as contrary to the logotherapeutic concept of self-transcendence—the human capacity to transcend oneself by engaging in values and meanings of the actual life.

For Frankl the central theme in therapy and counselling was always meaning. He developed logotherapy as a supplement to psychotherapy to help therapists to work with this human quest which patients and clients often raised. Logotherapy was developed explicitly to alleviate or "cure" the suffering caused by a loss of meaning in life or in specific situations. Experiencing loss of meaning can cause an "existential vacuum", as Frankl called it, and lead, according to him, to depression, addiction, and aggression.

This book

The book starts with a perspective on the role of emotions in our lives—a focus that became very central in modern existential analysis. It shows how feelings need to be taken seriously in order to have inner fulfilment in life. This emphasis marks a clear difference to Frankl's logotherapy, which is more about cognition (thinking) in the traditional sense.

This opening is followed by several papers on existential themes of happiness and meaning (including a meaning finding method), spirituality, time, fear, depression, suicidality, as well as child therapy and dealing with disability.

Existential analysis places great importance on understanding. We seek to understand the words of our clients, but also their background, fears, and possible options. It may also be very helpful for clients to understand their symptoms, and sometimes more important than to be rid of them. This involves an understanding of spoken and written language, but also body language, culture, and other forms of expression. Not only have I found significant interest and support for this approach in Western Europe and North America, but also in Australia, New Zealand, Estonia, Latvia, Lithuania, Sweden, Norway, South Africa, Indonesia, Malaysia, Thailand, and the Philippines. It strikes a chord with clients, carers, and clinicians, including specialists and generalists in psychology, psychiatry, emergency medicine, palliative care, pastoral care, social work and aboriginal health work.

I am honoured to be the co-editor of the English edition of this book, which has already been published in German, Spanish, Czech, and Russian. I am also delighted to be the lone "Anglo" contributor. You may still detect a certain continental "accent", but I hope you will find it inspiring and relevant, wherever you are.

Adelaide, 2015

References

Längle, A., & Probst, C. (Eds.) (1997). *Süchtig sein*. Wien: Facultas Universitätsverlag.

Wurm, C. S. E. (1991). *Definitionen, Diagnostik und Behandlung von alkoholbedingten Problemen. Süchtig sein. Entstehung, Formen und Behandlung von Abhängigkeiten*. Graz, Austria: Gesellschaft für Logotherapie und Existenzanalyse.

CHAPTER ONE

Can I rely on my feelings?

Alfried Längle

A strange question

Can people rely on their feelings? This might seem like a strange question. But in general do feelings have any noticeable significance? Do they play an important role in life or a more secondary role somewhat like a side effect—pleasant if we feel joy or happiness, disturbing if we feel anger, rage, jealousy, envy, fear, or depression?

Whether feelings are a side effect or not, many people regard them as a "solely private matter" and not something to be discussed in public. In an age of scientific and technological rationalism, feelings are often pejoratively referred to as the "stuff of the soul" and therefore something one should not pay too much attention to. That may be why the opinion that we should, "keep our feelings to ourselves", is so widespread. Feelings arise much like a motor being warmed by its own activity and can make a person *hot* if they are not *cooled* by reason. It is fashionable for many people to be *cool*, and therefore above and untouched by a situation. Feelings do not have any further significance for them, except that they point out certain tendencies and weaknesses. In this context, feelings are hidden, somewhat like our undergarments. Showing our feelings openly in public is, therefore, similar to

1

being caught in our underwear! This could prove quite embarrassing, perhaps even scandalous, and so many people deal with their emotions privately.

Others may regard feelings as an inner activity that occurs as a result of outward stimuli. Seen as a product of *outward stimulation*, feelings are much like ripples caused by a stone skipping across the water. For such people feelings are something alien, like a stone in a shoe that causes pressure or—in the best case—a tickle. These people are eager to get rid of feelings as soon as they arise. Feelings are experienced as pressure and "pushed away" to the outside. But how do you get rid of feelings? Feelings such as rage, anger, and joy are acted upon or played out in the immediate moment because the individuals believe that to keep their feelings in check or to keep their feelings to themselves would literally make them sick.

As we see from these introductory remarks, there are different conceptions of what feelings may mean to us and consequently there are different ways of dealing with them. It is not surprising that in our daily lives we sometimes don't know what to do with our feelings. It is not always easy to understand and to interpret them. It may sometimes be difficult to deal with them and to get along with their intensity and force, but also with the fact that they make us insecure, shocked, or hurt. The question that began this chapter, "Can (and may) I rely on my feelings?", is therefore worthy of exploration.

Behind our (often not further elaborated) *ideas* about emotions lie our *experiences* with the feelings. Our experiences with certain emotions, for example, may not have been consistently encouraging. If we have experienced being in love and following our hearts only to be subsequently rejected, the result may be that we develop a clouded or distorted idea about love or relationships.

It is not surprising that for many people *facts*—data, numbers, proofs, arguments and logical reflections—rather than emotional experiences, are considered reliable. To rely solely on feelings after such bad experiences would be considered out of touch with reality, like the behaviour of a naive, incurable, or idealistic romantic or mystic. The "hardliner" of reason would believe that placing a primacy on one's emotions is similar to making decisions by reading tea leaves. Such a person considers inner strength and personal success to be the outcome of rational, consistent, and logical strategies. Through these he can pursue his goals and achieve what he wants.

Emotions: a meaningful reality

The question remains whether feelings can be disregarded for a long time or if they are in fact a *power* that can make the heart pound and the hands shake of even the "coolest" and most rational person. Should feelings demand our attention?[1]

A closer look at emotions reveals the substantial part they play in human existence. A great part of our life takes place within our feelings. Our lives are saturated with emotions; they are present during our waking hours and even while we sleep and dream. Emotions are present from the very beginning of life until old age. Emotions make demands of us and ask us to deal with them to a certain degree. We may not even be conscious of the fact that emotions accompany every action we take and every experience, thought, and affect we have, both past and present. To experience anything in life is to feel emotion about something. And only when we truly feel do we experience. Emotions are the basis and power for motivation, and in this sense they carry with them and are the trigger for both the beginning and cessation of behaviour. One of the first things we notice when we wake up in the morning is the mood we are in. We might be joyful or sad, happy or annoyed, cheerful or angry.

Our entire waking condition until sleep sets in is carried by, and saturated with, moods. As mood and motivation, as power, and as background to experience, feelings are woven into every aspect of our lives. A person's biography is laden with patterns of emotions. This extends to biological life and the degree to which our bodies are formed and transformed by emotions. Feelings contribute to the form and contours of wrinkles in a face, the position of a head, or a person's posture. They speak about the states of feelings that have been dominant throughout the course of our lives. A patient once told me: "Against feelings reason is powerless," as she described being terrorised by fear for thirty-five years. The denial of feelings only leads to them hiding behind the power of the body. With the additional assistance of the body, feelings—now encoded—affect a person even more intensely. Buried feelings eventually reveal themselves in disturbed sleep, migraines, problems with digestion or breathing, and psychosomatic disturbances.

Owing to their constant presence and their tremendous influence on our lives, those of us who work in the field of psychology and therapy hold that feelings are just as real as the body we see before us. To overlook feelings, and the effect they have on us both psychologically and biologically, is akin to overlooking a patient's constant abuse of her body. Someone who never exercises, gets inadequate amounts of sleep, eats unhealthy food, drinks alcohol to excess, and smokes will, sooner or later, become sick. The body will eventually rebel. This is not so different from someone who constantly disregards her feelings by repressing them or keeping them suppressed through distractions such as excessive work, constant activity, or perhaps even drugs.

But it is not only the negative consequences that convey the power and significance that feelings have. Feelings are a *positive reality* in our lives as they are the bridge that enables closeness—closeness and relationships to people, to oneself, even to things and objects. This is because emotions constitute our *body of experience*. Only when we participate emotionally in life do we get anything substantial out of a the experience. Without the resonance of emotions, the world would remain flat and silent—music would have no sound, pictures no colour, and our memories would be pale and silent. Everything in life is revitalised through our experience and expression of emotions. Feelings bring life into our life. Feelings are the reason that we go to eat at a good restaurant, watch a particular movie, seek out and meet others. When the feelings lose their natural position, all must become more "extra-"—extraordinary, exotic, special—in order that a meal tastes, a movie gives pleasure, and an encounter is of value.

As central as emotions are to humankind, they are also somewhat *sinister*. This dimension of emotions is fleeting and intangible. Because of this, emotions have a different nature than the body, which is more tangible and predictable. In the West, we have been taught to see things objectively and to rely on that objectivity. Therefore our feelings seem rather frightening to us. Feelings fluctuate and moods can be unstable, changeable, freakish, labile, exorbitant, and, of course, purely subjective in their being and expression. We cannot count, weigh, or measure them reliably. It causes us to feel insecure when observing how feelings can change and, in fact, often we do not know why they change, or why they sometimes change so rapidly. Feelings arise from seemingly unknown and uncontrollable depths, stay with us for a while, and then disappear again; we do not know where they have gone. The minimal control we seem to have over them and the sense of being at their mercy can evoke fear. We cannot be apathetic about the commotion caused by our feelings, for they affect us deeply and dramatically. The feelings make us vulnerable; we can be insulted or hurt, feel stress or insecurity. On the other hand, we are also capable of feeling happy, joyful, cheerful, humorous, or hopeful on account of emotions.

* * *

A sixty-seven-year-old patient came into my care afraid that he was going to have another heart attack and therefore wanted to have his blood pressure checked. He had suffered a severe heart attack ten years prior and had been receiving his pension since then. The cause of his fear, however, was the stress and tension he had been experiencing because of his wife's decision to get a divorce. He had not expected his wife to be contemplating divorce, despite the fact that he had recently had extramarital relationswith a widow his age and expressed that for the first time in his life he was in love. He did not count with any attempt of divorce from his wife because she had always had affairs. Up until this time the relationships his wife had had were of no concern to him; he was not really conscious of them. But his wife was now taking the opportunity—it seemed for financial reasons—to get a divorce.

This man did not consult me for psychological reasons—not pain, anguish fear, worry, or insecurity about the future. These feelings were not tangible enough for him; they were not real enough. He wanted, rather, to have his body examined! My patient believed his feelings were subordinate to his physical welfare and of no real importance at all. This behaviour is both typical and widespread amongst those who do not know how to deal with the reality of their emotions.

After I had checked the man's blood pressure I spoke to him about his fear. I told him that his fear of another heart attack was understandable but that I was under the impression that his fear ran deeper than that. He agreed; at which point he said that ever since childhood he had lived in fear. In his profession he had always been afraid to trust his colleagues. He was always afraid of being disappointed. While talking about his fear of being disappointed he recalled a sentence his mother had often repeated. His mother, who had been a very energetic woman, had been to a renowned psychotherapist in Vienna for treatment when he was almost a year old. The therapist had advised: "One has got to keep the inexpressibly active women away from their children, out of fear that they might smother them." His mother had recited this sentence often in front of guests and friends. As a consequence, she had never caressed or held her children. Did she ever realise what this might have meant to her young son? He was hindered in the development of his emotional life and his basic trust was shaken.

The following excerpt from a conversation I had with this man reveals to some degree the outcome of the effect of this on his life and the inattentive manner in which he subsequently dealt with his emotions. In any of the talks we had he always viewed emotions as subordinate. I therefore asked him directly whether behind the difficult relationship he had with his energetic wife was perhaps a simultaneous longing for his energetic mother. At this point the sixty-seven-year-old man blushed and was noticeably moved. After uttering a few irrelevant words he composed himself and then in an objective manner stated that this had been so at that time and that one could not do anything about it now anyway. He did not feel any sadness on account of this. All of this had simply made him harder and more prone to logical thinking. He was thankful to his mother for this.

P: It really is of no use to have such feelings. It is only like self-pity.
TH: Self-pity, I would think, might be what you could now give yourself as compensation in lieu of what your mother did not provide: that you have feelings for yourself, that you yourself feel.
P: I do not want to do this.
TH: When you think this way you lock yourself in and are barred against many emotions.
P: People also say that I do not have any joy … Is it possible that there is a connection with my being afraid of emotions?
TH: There are many painful and sad feelings within …
P: Chaotic feelings, I would say, and much sensitivity … I can control thoughts, but feelings? That is why I always lived in the rational world. My wife almost went crazy on account of my logical analyses. I have always had trouble living out my emotions. I always felt emotions to be a nuisance.
TH: Perhaps you could not eliminate your emotions as much as you thought and, in the end, the feelings came to control you?
P: It is possible that this distanced basic mood, the pessimism and the fear, originate there. And that I had the constant feeling that my feelings would be disappointed.

I was moved by the encounter with this man. It made me sad to see him, at the age of sixty-seven-years, having suffered from his heart infarction and with his ruined marriage, and having so much fear inside him. In spite of his age and professional success, on the inside he remained that lonely and abandoned child he had been when he was two or three years old. If only he had had an opportunity earlier in his life to rely on his feelings! If he could have accepted his feelings of longing for his mother, if he could have cried! Instinctively I thought that had that been the case, his life would have taken a different course. The relationship he had with his wife, indeed with himself and his body, would not have been so distanced. What he lacked was in fact never that distant from him. He had felt the feelings he lacked in his childhood and now, in the present moment of therapy, he had blushed, revealing their secret presence. Who, I wondered, had told him that he could not have these feelings of longing, sadness, and fear? How much could someone have helped him by being interested in what the small boy had felt and sensed?

In order for us to have the courage to rely and depend on our feelings, we need the assistance and encouragement of other people from time to time, especially from those closest to us who understand us. The person who remains alone with his or her emotions will soon have to push them away in order not to be overwhelmed by them. Because my patient never felt that anyone took notice of the condition of his soul, he came to believe that it was important to shove aside any feelings he had. And this attitude was reinforced as he progressed from boyhood to manhood.

This man also showed that one can somehow remain alone in life, after all. This is helpful in situations in which there is no other way to escape, to survive. But if problems are pushed away and not addressed, they are not solved! My patient's physical condition, the direction his marriage took, and his falling in love late in life, were all indications that *his life* was not content the way it was. Because of his suffering and fear, his attention was focused on something that he himself could not understand.

Feelings as signposts and indicators: emotional states and moods as perceptions of our present life conditions

When we focus on the importance of emotions, it is equally important to look at the *limitations* of their significance. We are not always well served when we follow our feelings unrestrained. We must understand our feelings—a little—in order to know what they mean.

The patient described in the example above did the right thing on the one hand by not giving into his fears. He had shoved his feelings aside throughout his life. He could not have lived, had a family, or had a career had he acted on his fears and distrust. Given his emotional disposition and the fact that he had only himself to rely on, this man probably made the best possible choices for his life. He was successful because he distrusted his emotional states and produced a heavy reliance on logic alone. Once again, given his dominant feelings of fear and distrust, this was probably the best course of action. This was correct in his situation since the predominant feelings of angst and distrust were deduced feelings. They arose as a consequence of his suppressed longing for his mother, which he had never expressed. In turn, the suppression of the feelings caused him to lose touch with what was important to him. Specifically, the lack of motherly contact and the subsequent loss of a personal inner relationship produced feelings of insecurity. These feelings were strong enough that he felt as though the ground beneath his feet was neither stable nor secure. With his life surrounded by fear, insecurity, and a "basic feeling of distrust", his initial feelings of longing, loneliness, and helplessness were gradually lost.

Emotional states such as fear, general insecurity, distrust, doubts about one's self-worth, sadness, and loneliness should not, however, be followed blindly. The adage, "Fear is a bad advisor," is apt. These particular emotional states are different; they are *signs, indications, and warnings* that draw our attention to something. They illuminate our physical condition, psychological and biographical experiences. Somewhat like headlights, they give us information concerning our well-being. If I am unable to feel joy, for example, this could be an indication of physical exhaustion or an emotional memory of a period when I experienced sadness or stress. When these emotional states and moods arise, we should allow ourselves to follow these feelings from time to time and discover their origin in order to understand them.

My patient could have asked himself where his fears and distrust came from. Because he kept his emotions at a distance, he could not understand their importance and was therefore unable to ask about their origin. As paradoxical as it may sound, a person who is full of distrust is often too naive to place distrust where it would be appropriate; he was too credulous. The opposite of what is intended often occurs: the constant neglect of emotions inadvertently fuels emotions to reign supreme. At that point, feelings really are unrestrained and so they must be warded off, leaving us to shield ourselves even more. The more we overlook emotions, the less we understand them as signs indicating deep longings, deficits, and hurt that lie within our own lives.

How can this particular group of feelings be identified/recognised? This is a group of feelings that inform about the physical and psychological condition of a person. They can correlate with the immediate situation and, for example, perceive the oppressive stickiness of a room. Their purpose is to push towards an optimisation of the situational conditions because they are a precondition for a good guidance of life. But feelings can appear in the same shape/form/manner in very different and varying situations. Then they are largely decoupled from the outer situation. Nevertheless, they are signposts. They point to conditions—but now to conditions that are not in the given situation but stem from the past, and which now have only to be searched and understood. These conditions at what rely the repetitive or continuous feelings or moods lie within the person. They are often disturbing in the situation and not easily understood; they are nevertheless of worth and significance. Any attempt to locate their cause outside of us is fruitless and distracting. We need to pay attention to them because they include important pieces of information, especially if they repeat themselves.

In a concrete situation where intense feelings of fear emerge, for example, it is often better to deal with them by distancing ourselves, in order to manage the situation. Feelings that overtake a person suddenly on the street, at home, or at work are likely not connected to the immediate situation or location. The feelings have instead been *smuggled* into the situation. Fears such as these have to do with us, with our bodily condition, or with a neurotic disturbance. Similarly, strong feelings of distrust can also be a sign or indicator but are unlikely to be connected to a specific situation, if, for example, no concrete collaborator gives rise to distrust. When we only find general answers like "one can never be sure", then the feelings we have refer to inner conditions of the past. Then we should follow them betimes to find the trace of the origin of these feelings.

Yet another example can be found in the recurrent feeling that "everyone else is better than I am". This is an emotional state that we should not aspire to. It is paralysing. It is important to gain some distance from a depressive feeling such as this in order to remain capable of living. However, even with a temporary distancing from such a feeling, we should see it as a sign or indicator that points to something deeper. The origins or conditions for such feelings need to be discovered. We can conduct this search or discovery by ourselves, though it is even better through dialogue with an understanding person, a friend, or even with a psychotherapist. Sadly, a person who has the feeling that everyone else is better than her often believes this herself at a profoundly deep level. Nonetheless, such a person hopes that this is in fact not true and she will fight against this feeling with all her might. She will typically fight the feeling by sacrificing herself for others to the point of exhaustion. She will come to believe that these constant acts of sacrifice will in fact save her from these feelings of inferiority. In reality, this behaviour demands great effort and causes tremendous stress.

These actions are understandable to a degree, because it is often too painful for the individual to search out and confront the original cause of such feelings. In confronting the origin of these emotions, an individual may have to relive how often he felt judged by fellow pupils, siblings, or neighbours; how often his efforts and achievements were disregarded; or how often his parents gave him the impression—or even explicitly stated—that his life was a burden on them. When experiences are seen from this perspective, how can anything a person does be considered good when he has the feeling that it is bad that he should even exist? Emotions are far-reaching and this is why treatment has to also delve into these depths.

I was often impressed and moved when I became witness during my talks and therapies to the enormous achievements that people have accomplished in their fight against inner desperation and the influence such feelings have had on their lives. Sometimes they have carried these feelings with them for years, if not decades, and yet they have also pushed through their lives. They live out their work and leisure time, endure their crying and desperation, until they come to a dead end and finally consult someone for help. In hearing these people's stories, I have often wished that they had started treatment much earlier. But I can respect their efforts, distancing themselves from the burden of these emotions in order to live.

We must remember though that anyone who believes they have triumphed over stressful emotions on their own often develops a negative position or attitude towards all their emotions and will be opposed to any course of psychotherapy. These people are very often preoccupied with fighting their feelings, rather than interested in understanding or discovering their origins through discussion. Because the fear of emotions is so strong, the signs pointing to something deeper are viewed solely as a threat and thereby misinterpreted. And really it is a threat, which can be felt for a certain period of time during treatment very strongly and painfully. But left unexamined and not understood, the feeling of threat itself is a burden, dangerous and incalculably. Because these feelings push towards being understood in order that they can be better—and more realistically—adapted to the living conditions of the particular individual. These feelings literally challenge a person to take a position towards them and to deal with them in a realistic manner. This is the purpose of such enduring, repetitive, and burdensome feelings.

Help in dealing with emotional states

Quite often our emotional states are not serious enough that they require therapeutic help. In many cases people are quite capable of finding an appropriate orientation amidst the *forest of emotional indicators* on their own. There is a simple *method* that can be used to put some distance between ourselves and the kinds of recurring feelings that hinder us in our daily lives, unless they are not too strong. This procedure involves three times a taking a position to procure the individual a personal stand in regard to his or her feelings:

1. First, a position is taken towards the **outside**, towards the world which is threatening, burdening, or boxing in. Therefore, the first step in confronting the emotion is not to observe the emotion but rather to observe the external situation. We are checking what possible connections there are between the outside or external world and the emotion we are experiencing. For example, we experience the feeling that everyone else is better than us. Taking a position towards the outside world, we must ask ourselves: "Is this really true? How can I be sure of this?" Or, if we have feelings of distrust, we need to question whether the emotion is appropriate in this situation: "Does this correspond to what I do see? Is this feeling appropriate to this situation?". Only after we have opened our eyes and allowed ourselves to perceive the reality of the outside world can we move forward and observe the feelings we have inside.

2. Confronting the emotion now leads to examining the position taken towards the **inside**, to take the position towards ourselves and our

feelings. We want to become clear about the consequences in the case that our feelings would be correct. We ask: "Could I bear and endure these feelings? What would actually happen?

The position we take towards the inside, towards our own emotional state, relates to the questions: "If this really is the reality, what would the consequences be for me? If others really were better than me at skiing or playing cards, what would actually happen? Would *I* lose something? Could I bear this?" Or, on the other hand, when the feelings are considered to be right: "Could I bear these feelings of distrust or insecurity for one day or in this particular situation?"

3. Once we have freed ourselves realistically from the outside and from the inside and secured ourselves so far, we can determine our individual position more objectively by asking: "What is at stake right now? What matters to me?" By working through the previous two steps and gaining a sense of security, we become free for this step. We have now to take a **position to the positive**: "Am I actually trying to be better than everyone else or is this about my simply wanting to go for skiing?" "Is this about being free from feelings of distrust or about getting my work done in a certain fashion?" By turning towards the positive, which should in fact be our main concern, we are able to stand on our ground again. The goal of this method is to regain an inner position, and it is therefore called the *personal position method* (Längle, 1994, pp. 6–21).

Up until now we have looked at a group of feelings that contain hints to our needs and how to deal with ourselves—feelings that check whether we are caring well for ourselves or if we are neglecting our life. However, such emotional states do not give us ground and do not provide orientation for further-reaching decisions though. They originate within us and apply to us, but they do not indicate the meaning of a situation. They mirror and reflect physical, psychological, as well as the life history or "biographical" conditions of an individual. These feelings remain with us because they belong to us. Feelings connect us to our body and our history. They form a relationship with the present conditions of the outer situation. In this sense, they have a *referential character*. They challenge us to both search for and understand what they mean. Understanding our feelings means to better understand ourselves.—But because these feelings do not always relate directly to a situation at work, within the family, or a conversation we are currently engaged in, it is important at times to keep a certain distance from them. Our lives would dissolve if we entertained every mood swing, every fit of anger and rage, every disappointment or joyous feeling. A certain distance from these feelings also protects us from wallowing in them or from a pathological tendency to *bathe in emotional pain*. Sentimentality is logically the result when we do not understand our states of feeling as signposts but as goals—states in which we want to remain.

Emotions as a scent: the "intuitive feeling" for what is essential (right)

There is another group of emotions that reverberates within us like a sound or tone and occurs when we *turn towards another human being or an object*. This emotional tone is very well known to us and is always present in everything we do or carefully observe. Quite often the tone is not immediately perceived but overlooked or thrown into a pot with other emotional conditions and then set aside. But this tone has a different origin than the first group of emotions we examined. It develops within the reality of the outer or external situation. This situation causes its sound. This tone is like the accompanying music to the outer reality, like *an inner picture of the outer reality*. Because this picture originates on the outside, it coincides contemporarily *beside* our internal emotional states. We can, for example, have a fearful emotional state and yet pay attention to what we feel while we are also eating and enjoying our meal. To a certain degree we can be captivated by a book, enjoy a concert, avidly follow a speech or be engrossed in a film without notice or concern for the emotions we initially came into the activity with. When the experiences are suspenseful, we might even forget to some extent how we are and not be observant of our emotional state. While observing the film we *feel* the story, we experience and feel what is going on *out there*.

Because this process is so important in making life rich, precious, and fulfilling, the steps should be examined in greater detail. What do we actually do when we watch a movie, for example? We hear, watch, and think. Many things are happening during this process. When we turn our attention towards someone else or something other than ourselves, we create a condition of *openness* within ourselves. Our eyes and ears, sometimes even our mouths, are open to an experience. Much like the eye that lets in light by opening the pupil, we similarly allow something to enter us through the openness of the soul when we turn our attention and interest outward. What is it that reaches us through our openness? What is it that touches and moves us? These are *existential values*. We feel that the story is thrilling, grasping, touching. We feel this in varying degrees and it can change from one moment to the next. We feel both the good and the bad, we feel what is important for life yet also what alienates us from it. In an encounter with another human being we can feel many things simultaneously: how another person is inclined towards us or how we are towards her, whether we like this other person or whether she likes us, or the extent to which we get along with one another.

It is amazing what can be sensed through language, sight, and sound. But we in fact can feel even more than the qualities and tensions. If we are open towards ourselves in this process, we are also capable of feeling and sensing our personal inner position towards what is observed. We can sense, feel, and be aware of our intuitive position about what is in front of us, aware of what we may dismiss or what we might agree on. Initially we sense all of this emotionally. We then deal with it through thought. We feel or sense our inner positions followed by our initial instructions for action, for example, how I should behave towards this person, if I want to stay or leave this situation, what I should actually say or do.

This second category of emotions makes it clear to us what is *required in the present moment*. They *unmask a situation regarding its existential value*. What we get to feel is what is essential, what is important and what *makes sense*. These emotions are a personal orientation and they direct us towards what is to be done and what is the *right* action for now. They have a *directive* quality. These feelings are far more sensitive than the logical mind is sharp-witted. In that sense, Frankl (1970, p. 95) interpreted Pascal's saying, "The heart has reasons which are unknown to reason," to suggest that what is really essential is not perceptible to the eye and mind. Antoine de Saint-Exupéry stated in *The Little Prince*, "One can only see right with the heart. The essentials are imperceptible to the eye" (1988, p. 72).[2] What we can feel and sense with our hearts far exceeds what we are able to grasp with our minds. We have difficulty understanding this *sixth sense* because it may look sometimes like clairvoyance, our feeling perceiving something, long before it takes place.

The following example illustrates this point. A woman had conflicted thoughts about whether she should move away with her two children.

She felt that it was no longer beneficial for her and the children to remain in the home. Her husband showed no understanding of her problem and did not respond to her feelings and reflections. The woman became more and more oppressed by her life-conditions, despite the husband's belief that she had no reason to feel oppressed or to contemplate moving away. He believed that everything was in order and that she and the children were well taken care of. It was true: she and the children were well looked after. But, despite this fact, the feeling became stronger and stronger that soon she would not be able to live any longer under the present circumstances. She eventually decided to move away. She took the children with her. The husband remained by himself. She sensed that she had done the right thing, although she came into great need and also experienced doubt yet almost despair. Had she made a biggest mistake of her life? She endured these doubts and suffered from bitter distress and exhaustion for years. She never met her husband again. This woman sensed intuitively that it was necessary for her to leave the marriage and she followed her feeling. She had the courage to rely on her feelings and thus ultimately on herself. She felt the necessity. These events took place in 1938. The woman, Anna Lambert, was a Jew and her husband an Austrian. She and her children left Austria for England. Her sister, who remained, died in a concentration camp. She describes her story in a book with the accurate title *You Cannot Run Away From Anything* (Lambert, 1992).

It often requires a great deal of strength and courage to depend on your own intuitive feelings, as it did for Anna Lambert. Anyone who is able to rely on their intuition and successfully manage to live in harmony with their feelings has achieved a biographical masterpiece. This accomplishment need not be spectacular, and it can also be accompanied, as we saw in this illustration, by much effort and sorrow. However, when we are successful in following the path that we feel is right, important, and necessary, we truly live *our life*. And only then do we live our life. Can we remain true to ourselves if we live contrary to our own perceptions?

But where do people learn to rely on themselves, on their intuition, on their feelings? Who told me in childhood to trust my feelings and instincts? Who supported me in looking at what I personally feel and sense? We should reconsider how we raise children, the pedagogy we use in child development, and look for ways and approaches that promote the respect for intuitive feeling and perception. An education that considers the best interests of children will promote the importance of intuitive feelings. *The person who has never learned to live by what is important to him has not learned to live but merely to obey!* The person who cannot feel what is important to him cannot rely on his feelings and ultimately becomes alienated from his true self. If I cannot rely on my own feelings, how will I form my decisions? Who will guide me in the countless situations I encounter in life and the directions I should pursue?—In order to discover the true orientation of one's life, it is important to rely on our feelings. Otherwise we become dependent on rules, external authorities, or passing trends to tell us what to do.

Living your own life: a case study

During the course of our daily routines, it is easy not to pay much attention to our intuitive feelings. We are quick to follow public opinion or perhaps what we have been taught or what someone has ordered us to do. We might give in to our fears or the constraints of what seems to be a hopeless situation. Men, for example, often state that they are forced to follow only facts or the demands of their professions according to claims of "reason". Women often tell me that they would sooner follow the expectations and conventions of society.

A typical example of this is Klara. She is thirty-seven years old. She is well-liked by everyone, easy to get along with, and married with two children. Everything seems to fit in her life and no one would think she has any problems. Her life, while outwardly rich with activities and social events, is in fact empty on the inside. Klara believes she is superficial. She is unhappy and feels as though she has lived in a dream world up until now. She has always had the feeling that her feelings are not right, and as a consequence she has always adapted to the demands of the outer world. This constant adaptation has resulted in her losing a relationship with her own emotions. She behaves in a certain way simply to please others. She believes the person she is, is not good enough and she does not know what she wants in life. On the other hand, she has an acute sense of what others demand of her. Her life is characterised by ambition, assimilation, and function.

Klara felt this way even as a child. Her parents valued only top performances in school. The things she did on her own while playing or using her imagination where never recognised. Praise and critique was only given to her other siblings. Klara was inconspicuous; she was always well behaved, industrious, and never at fault. She was so well adapted, in fact, that no one noticed her.

Klara now lives with the feeling that her life has been going on without her. She rarely makes a decision or takes a stand towards anything. She is unable to say to herself, "This is good." Her statements are negatively formulated and thus they serve as a veil. If she likes something she says: "That's *not bad*." If something is "not bad", she can assure herself that she has not taken a clear and decisive position. So she remains flexible and can easily adapt in order to share the same opinion as someone else, something she couldn't do if she definitively stated: "This is good. I like it!" In a deeper sense, she has taken the road of least possible resistance. And yet she admits, "I am losing myself in the process because I am not taking myself seriously anymore." The housework and children are boring to her; they are simply a duty. She cannot speak to anyone about this because she believes her feelings are wrong. As a result, Klara sticks to a cliché of womanhood: a real woman does the laundry enthusiastically; she is happy when the children come home from school so she can help them with their homework. As long as Klara lives this way, or so she thinks, it is possible for her to take herself seriously as a woman.

For years now Klara has tried to be happy and to accommodate herself to these demands. But, in spite of all the effort, she has never felt happy. The more she tries to accommodate herself, the less attention she pays to what she likes about herself and what is important to her. Her own intuitive feelings to do what is right in her eyes are lost underneath duties, demands, and expectations. She increasingly feels her life to be void of meaning, and this in spite of all the effort she has made and duties she has taken on.

Only when she began to let go of "what was supposed to be important to a woman" and to pay a bit of attention to what *she* liked, what she felt was in fact good and right, did her life begin to become exciting and interesting for her. It became thrilling but also tense and troublesome. She had first to learn to discover her intuitive feelings, to realise and become aware of them and, finally, to give them room for expression. Gradually she began to live according to her feelings, regardless of whether she received appreciation for it and whether or not it was recognized as an accomplishment. These personal gains, however, led to tensions within the family. Her family had become accustomed to a woman who had always adapted to, and functioned for, them and now had to readjust. It is very understandable that Klara often became anxious and felt insecure in her new trials. But, in spite of these feelings, she increasingly began to live the way she wanted to: with her children, in her marriage, and in her leisure time.

Her method centred on the following questions, which she now always put forward prior to any activity: "Do I *like* to do this, or am I doing it just because of pressure from other people?" "Am I doing it because I want to achieve recognition?" "Am I trying to just function smoothly?" "Am I trying to appease the demands of others?" Klara was in her late thirties when she gradually learned to live her own life. *Her life* became defined by what she sensed to be right, important, and precious. In accordance with a pivotal question within existential analysis, she often asked in the midst of her daily life: "Do I like to live the way I am living? And if this is not the case, what can I do, or not do, *today* in order to live the way I like to tomorrow?"

Outlook

The ideas I have presented here are applicable to both men and women. There are, of course, differences in emotionality between men and women just as there are between all human beings in general. This must be the case since *emotional states* are the manifestations of an individual's inner reality, especially one's physical reality and condition, and unique life history. Since the gender type is also related to the feeling of the body (which is different between sexes) emotional states may differ between sexes and maybe as much between different typologies of bodies.

Gender or physical differences are not apparent in the second group of *"intuitive feelings"*. The ability to sense what is personally important in a given situation appears to be independent from sex. In fact, during several examinations on this issue (illustrated in the large-scale examination of Christa Orgler, 1990) no significant difference between the genders was established. Men and women appear to be equal when it comes to their emotional capacity and ability to grasp what makes sense for them in a given situation.

The distinction between feelings that we have presented here is rarely made. But it makes a remarkable difference depending on whether a feeling is a sign or an indication that connects us to our well-being and to the past, or whether it is a perception of the present situation and forms, as such, a basis for decision-making and direction for the future life. Knowing what the feeling is connected to and separating it from our present condition is fundamentally important. It provides a basis for decision-making and a direction for constructive living. Conversely, the person who relies on his emotional states, who gives them priority, and allows them unrestrained expression, will not experience a fulfilling existence. Such a person gets trapped in an *ego trip* of sentiments and becomes unbearable to both himself and to others. In order to make decisions and choices about our future, watching our emotions and trusting our own intuitive sense about *what is right* provides a reliable foundation. We need to rely on this intuitive sensing, otherwise we run the very real risk of alienating ourselves from ourselves and others. We have the choice but the consequences will "have us". But don't step over our states of feelings! If we do not attempt to understand the origin of our feeling-states, our lives will remain bound to our own unattended physical and biographical status. Unattended, these emotional states will begin to twist our view of the world and cloud our ability to intuitively feel. Emotional states belong to the body of human life and provide the background for our experiences and life's overall continuity. These states need to be taken care of and understood.

You may be familiar with the saying, "Pay attention or pay the consequences". After this examination we could alter this saying slightly in order to express the relation between these two emotional types: "Pay attention to your intuitions or you *must feel* the consequences." People who are not open to the uniqueness and preciousness of each situation will soon feel an emptiness which will also burden their well-being and their mood.

People who can rely on their feelings, however, are never alone; they always have at least one person with themselves: themselves.

Notes

1. The terms emotion and feeling are used in a comparable way in this article. In the scientific literature in EA the term feeling, though, stands for the most general understanding of all forms of feelings, whereas emotions means intimate, personal feelings arising as an intimate answer (like joy or love). Affects, instead, are stimulated, psychodynamic feelings (like aggression, fear, eroticism). Other forms of feelings are mood (long-lasting feelings) and tickle (Längle, 2003).

2. Frankl (1970, p. 95) interpreted Pascal's phrase "Le coeur a ses raisons que la raison no connaît point," as: "Sometimes the wisdom of our hearts proves to be deeper than the insight of our brains."

References

Frankl, V. (1970). *The Will to Meaning: Foundations and Applications of Logotherapy*. New York: New American Library.

Lambert, A. (1992). *Du kannst vor nichts davonlaufen*. Wien: Picus.

Längle, A. (1994). Personale Positionsfindung. *Bulletin der GLE, 11*: 6–21.

Längle, A. (2003). Zur Begrifflichkeit der Emotionsbegriffe in der Existenzanalyse. In: A. Längle (Ed.), *Emotion und Existenz* (pp. 185–200). Wien: WUV-Facultas.

Orgler, Ch. (1990). *Die existenzanalytische Anthropologie als ätiologischer Erklärungsbeitrag für psychopathologische Prozess*. Die Existenz-Skala—eine Validierungsstudie im Gesundheitsbereich. Dissertation an der Universität Wien.

Saint-Exupéry, A. (1998). *Der kleine Prinz*. Zürich: Arche.

Further reading

Längle, A. (1992). Ist Kultur machbar? Die Bedürfnisse des heutigen Menschen und die Erwachsenenbildung. In: *Kongressband „Kulturträger im Dorf"* (pp. 65–73). Bozen: Auton. Provinz, Assessorat für Unterricht und Kultur.

Längle, A. (1993). (Ed.) *Wertbegegnung: Phänomene und methodische Zugänge*. Wien: GLE—Verlag.

Längle, A. (1993). Glossar zu den Emotionsbegriffen, ibid. 161–173.

Längle, A. (2003). (Ed.) *Emotion und Existenz*. Wien: WUV-Facultas.

Längle, A. (2003). Wertberührung—Bedeutung und Wirkung des Fühlens in der existenzanalytischen Therapie. In: A. Längle (Ed.), *Emotion und Existenz* (pp. 49–76). Wien: WUV-Facultas.

Längle, A. (2010). Gefühle—erwachtes Leben: Zur Begründung und Praxis einer existenzanalytischen Emotionstheorie. *Existenzanalyse, 27*: 59–71.

Längle, A. (2011). Emotionality: An existential-analytical understanding and practice. In: R. Trnka, K. Balcar, & M. Kuska (Eds.), (2013). *Re-constructing Emotional Spaces: From Experience to Regulation* (pp. 57–86). Saarbrücken: Lambert Academic Publishing.

CHAPTER TWO

Meaning and happiness: on the vital significance of meaning

Christoph Kolbe

There is a longing inside every person to experience happiness. In fact, it is a special treat if we are able to say, "I am happy!" Further, it seems to be the case that the experience of happiness revives the experience of meaning.

In addition to defining the relationship between meaning and happiness, this chapter intends to deal with the inner conditions and attitudes that make it possible for happiness to find us. It is a worthwhile task to examine the outer living conditions and discover the effects that either promote or hinder our happiness.

When we deal with the insights on happiness that scientific analysis has provided us with, the existential analyst experiences something interesting: the attitudes and positions of a person who claims to be happy correlate in many ways to existential-analytic anthropology. This is why the results of many scientific analyses seem so familiar. A difference does remain however: from an existential analytic and logotherapeutic perspective, these insights are associated with the area of meaning. At least it seems this way with respect to the *positions and preconditions* that a person possesses concerning the world. There seems to be a high affinity between happiness and meaning. The following is intended to motivate, revive, and vitalise discussions on the question of happiness and meaning.

Let us begin with several personal questions. When was the last time you were truly happy? Was it a long time ago, or was it recently? What was it that made you so happy? Let us make the contrast clearer: Is there something meaningful in your life and day-to-day living that also makes you happy? Or is it meaningful but its association with happiness has long since passed? Does it now have more to do with necessity, thankfulness, or gratitude? Perhaps by the end of this chapter it will be possible for you to see the somewhat stale meaningfulness of life from a new point of view and to see a new quality of life from the standpoint of happiness. Perhaps you will experience yourself as livelier, fresher, and more vitalised—in any event, you will hopefully experience a broader connection to these specific "uplifting emotions".

A Chinese proverb (compare also Ernst, 1997, p. 21) addresses "happiness" as follows:

> If you want to be happy for an hour, get drunk.
> If you want to be happy for three days, marry.
> If you want to be happy forever, become a gardener.

This saying makes it wonderfully clear that there are different forms of happiness. There is short-term happiness which makes us forget everything around us for a moment, although this form of happiness is sometimes followed by grief. There are the large, distinguished experiences in life, such as a wedding and then the honeymoon, the passing of an important exam, or the landing of an important and desired job, indeed, any events in life that leave an impression on us for a long period of time, events that make us float in the air until we gradually land back in our ordinary lives. Then, there are the experiences one could characterise as bringing somewhat quieter, more subdued happiness to our lives, experiences that make an enduring experience of happiness possible. Through these experiences we know we are embedded in the laws of life. Just as there is spring, summer, autumn, and winter, there are times when we sow seeds onto the fields of our lives. We sow, accompany the growing process, and reap a harvest. And this takes place in every period of life with differing demands and themes. A gardener lives in harmony with these rhythms, knows what to do, and looks forward to each phase. Do we live in harmony with our rhythms of life? Can we say "yes" to them? Or are we enemies to these rhythms; do we aggravate them? How do we productively handle these laws in order to experience happiness?

Some may sceptically question whether happiness is in fact simply the drifting off into an egocentric individualism. One might respond, however, by asking, does the question of happiness not originate from a deeper longing within each person? Because we so seldom experience happiness or perceive it as endangered, we ban the question from our thoughts and instead transport it to the realm of idealistic dreams, preferring to call ourselves sovereign realists.

We might step further and ask, is happiness a far too spontaneous and incalculable phenomenon of chance? And, do we view happiness with some suspicion because of the pain we feel when it leaves us? Nonetheless, as humans we long, in our innermost being, to experience happiness and to be able to be happy. Perhaps we are far too vulnerable and lack the necessary knowledge to address the issue of longing.

We all have our experiences with happiness. I want to reflect upon the background and attitudes that underlie these experiences. Upon reflection, we may then ask, can a person do something in order to be happy? Can a person even learn to be happy? A question such as this contains within it the *provocative theses that we influence the manifestation of happiness in our lives!* From this perspective, I imagine happiness to be a person who searches for a home and decides to stay in a good place where it is pleasurable to stay. I also believe that as humans we can do something in order to experience happiness! The opposite is therefore true as well: if we do the wrong thing, we can drive happiness away.

It is certainly not the case that I can, or in fact want to, tell you in absolute terms the right thing to do in order to be happy! That would be arrogant of me. Certain insights remain, nonetheless, which—if the person in question takes them to heart—make it possible for happiness to remain in his or her life.

So far we can establish two significant factors of happiness:

1. *It is the unique character of happiness that makes it seem as though it falls into our laps.* Happiness feels as though it somehow enters our lives through a door from the outside, otherwise unavailable to us. This is the passive aspect of experiencing happiness.
2. *We can open ourselves up to happiness if it wants to meet us.* Søren Kierkegaard once said: "The door to happiness opens to the outside."

In other words, we can in fact do something to cause a stir in our lives, thereby opening ourselves to receive happiness.

But how do we open the door of our lives when happiness comes knocking? Let us begin with the basic question:

What is happiness?

Scientists categorise happiness as a *"higher emotion within the field of moods"*. For the majority of people, happiness is an explicit, positive emotion (compare Kast, 1997, pp. 16–23) similar to the feelings of joy, hope, and enthusiasm. Further, these feelings give us strength and vitality. The feeling of happiness is, however, more than a psychological need! Happiness is *the result of a certain experience or an attitude towards life.*

Happiness by definition is the "lasting realization of a fulfilled, meaningful and pleasant life" (David Myers in Ernst, 1997, p. 22). It is a mood in which one feels light, joyful, moved, and vitalised. We have two expressions in German that convey this: "We want to embrace the whole world because we are so happy," and, "Happiness makes us want to jump up and down." These descriptions of happiness come close to those within existential analysis. Existential analysis differentiates between two basic dimensions in the experience of every person. The first dimension takes into account whether we experience something as pleasant or unpleasant. This is the so-called psychological dimension of experience. The second dimension is the existential dimension where we experience something as fitting, good, or right for ourselves. A typical example of this differentiation is the general experience of someone not agreeing with you, yet you wanting to say something important to this person; you experience your heart beating fast and you feel a little afraid. The psychological experience is fear, but an inner knowledge indicates that something else is important or true and it is activated in spite of the fear. Frankl calls this state of events the "psycho-noetic antagonism" (Frankl, 1984, p. 148). Within the experience of happiness, the experience that something fits and is good, right, and important connects in a special way with our experiencing something as beautiful and pleasant. People speak of happiness when they are fulfilled by what is right and important to them, so much so that even a mood disturbance does little to affect this basic feeling of appropriateness.

Happiness, according to existential analysis, needs *reasons* (Frankl, 1982, p. 20). It is not only a mood in itself, it is the connection to something that causes happiness (compare also Kast, 1997, p. 47). The same is true for the experience of meaning.

It appears to be the case that the issue of happiness revives the issue of meaning. Meaning becomes livelier, richer, and fuller if it is lived within the horizon of happiness rather than remaining in the field of abstractions, principles, and purely cognitive processes, separated from emotion. It is exactly this point that has led to further developments in the understanding of existential analysis held by the GLE (Gesellschaft für Logotherapie und Existenzanalyse—"The International Society for Logotherapy and Existential Analysis"): the recollection of the emotional constitution of humanity when a person encounters the world and its question of meaning.

In Frankl's traditional logotherapeutic approach, the relationship between meaning and happiness is somewhat tense: "It is exactly the person who is overly ambitious about achieving happiness who, thereby, blocks the path to happiness for himself. So in the end all ambition for happiness … bears an impossibility within itself" (Frankl, 1985, p. 53). Elsewhere Frankl states that "the basic, natural ambition for mankind is the achievement of happiness", but that this is a prejudice that can be overcome (Frankl, 1982, p. 20). Elsewhere Frankl calls it a prejudice that has to be overcome, "that the human being ultimately strives to be happy" (Frankl, 1982, p. 20). From this perspective, should a person feel strange if he has within himself a longing for some happiness in his life? Is it a sign of psychological immaturity, according to this traditional view within logotherapy, to desire a life of simple happiness and light-heartedness?

It is important though not to misunderstand Frankl's views. Perhaps we should free him from a somewhat rigorous interpretation of his statements and what they seem to imply. Frankl is of course right when he says that people search for a *reason* to be happy. It is the unique character of happiness that it derives its achievement through reasons. We are joyful, for example, because of, or about, something. But this experience cannot lead us to disregard our need of, or ambition for, happiness. When we talk about happiness, we mean an intentional ambition, not simply the joyful emotional state. And this coincides with scientific analyses on happiness. The scientists differentiate between the mode of characteristics and the mode of the present state.

We could provocatively state: human beings cannot strive towards happiness directly (because it is the result of the achievement of values), but each individual can do a great deal to prepare a home for it. Happiness is given a chance to thrive when we adopt the right attitude towards life. Life is then not only meaningful, but also rich, fulfilled, and happy.

Preconditions and attitudes for personal happiness

One could also ask, what is the difference between happy and less happy people? What kind of characteristics can be found if one examines the experiences of people who say they are happy? The following characteristics can be named (see also Ernst, 1997, pp. 22–24):

1. **Happy people perceive themselves as designers**.
   Even more, they perceive themselves as creators of their lives. Good and bad things do not simply happen to these people as strokes of fate. They experience themselves more as *acting people within their circumstances*. In this sense, they know themselves to be creators and masters of their lives. Life does not just happen to them. They tend not to feel at the mercy of life, but recognise their own possibilities for design and see the open space around them. They recognise possibilities within their particular circumstances and subsequently change or accommodate themselves. They live out their lives in a basic movement of active effort through self-sacrifice. Within existential analysis we describe this attitude as *Acting*—in contrast to the attitude of *reacting*.

   The acting person experiences himself or herself as free and autonomous. In fact, a deep mystery of life is revealed through the experiences of such people: they experience themselves as involved, vitalised, and lively because, as Frankl states, they are immersed in the movement of acting in, and answering to, life. In these circumstances we experience ourselves existentially. By contrast, our lives become pale, meaningless, perhaps even boring, when we experience ourselves simply reacting to circumstances. In these cases, without our individual approach or unique answer to life, we simply function.

   Psychological disturbances are essentially characterised by patterns of reaction. We react to a stimulus with a certain pattern of behaviour. If we experience ourselves in our daily work as mere reactors when, for example, the desk is full of uncompleted work, the boss has given new orders, or the children are hungry, the inner experience being portrayed is one of passivity, even if a person is busy and doing many things. The same activities, however, can be done in an active and designing manner. The inner experience will then change for the individual to one that is active and positive: I am doing this action. I want to do something. And not: I have to do something. It seems to be an art of living that enables a person to adopt this kind of attitude. You should try this out the next time you have to sweep or clean the stairs, or the next time you want to sweep or clean them!

This experience gets support from another angle. One can observe that a so-called "stroke of good fortune" (winning the lottery, for example) only lifts a person's spirits for a short time. After a year, sometimes after a few weeks, these same people tend to revert to their normal, or even sub-normal, levels of happiness.

2. **Happy people desire to have what they get.**
Or, stated the other way round, "Happiness is not getting what you want, but wanting what you get" (Ernst, 1997, p. 22).

Hidden within this beautiful and witty saying lies another deep mystery of life, one we quite often do not like to face. Most people live with the attitude that life owes them the fulfilment of their wishes and that they have a right to this. Such people often state, "If I get this and that, then I can be content and happy." Of course we can have all sorts of expectations concerning life, but every further expectation brings us into deeper trouble. Life becomes increasingly constrained because it must be a certain way—the way we want it to be. What law states, however, that we have a right to have our wishes fulfilled? It is a dangerous thing to let our wishes and expectations take control. This speaks to our ability to practise the art of letting go and turning our attention to something else.

The following is an *example* of the problems caused by an attitude of expectation. You have completed a full day of work; you are looking forward to a few hours of leisure and are hoping that your partner at home has cooked something nice, has a bit of time to talk, and that the both of you can enjoy some hard-earned leisure time together. Instead of the expected scenario, you hear the sound of your partner's voice from the children's room while opening the door: "Hello honey! By the way, someone still has to go shopping. Why don't you figure out what we should eat for dinner; I am still taking care of the kids." How might a scene like this continue in your home? Or does a situation like this never occur because everyone simply adapts themselves and never consciously expresses their expectations. If that is the case, you need only wait until the children are a bit older …!

Or here is a different example, which you are all probably familiar with. You want to go on your annual vacation and hope the weather will be nice for various excursions. You arrive at your destination and the rain is pouring down. In fact it remains that way. How would you normally react to such a situation? Our thesis, as you will remember, is, happy people desire to have what they get!

If you can prepare for such unwanted events and situations, then there is a moment of freedom. An expectation has not yet been fixed in a stringent attitude. Expectations become a problem for community living and for encountering the world when they leave no room for other people. In such cases, expectations simply box us in by prescribing how something should be. It is precisely because of these hardened attitudes that we cannot bear it when something cannot be changed. This again belongs to the art of living. We all continue to have expectations, but *it is important to adapt our expectations to the challenges of a changed situation without immediately complaining about a loss.* And it is also important not to let expectations become an entrenched attitude of expectation.

As a psychotherapist, I am well aware that it is not always easy to let go of expectations—especially when people have had to undergo significant change. But this is where legitimate human needs can take on the characteristic of *neediness* for the adult person. At that point it is even harder to let go of our wishes and expectations. When we are in a place where we are well taken care of and sufficiently secure, we can be at ease with ourselves and accept the situation as it really is.

I would like to illustrate an *exercise* that can help you to handle expectations. The next time you come home from work and wish to have a comfortable evening at home, take a moment while your hand is still on the handle of the door. Become conscious of your wishes, your hopes and ideas about the evening. And then say to yourself: "Maybe it will all be completely different."

The results of scientific analyses on happiness go a step further: it is not only about letting go of expectations, but also about saying "yes" to that which is actually there. This forms an attitude of potential happiness. Is this statement not an incredibly unreasonable demand? Is there no other way to find peace? Why is this? By desiring what we get, we give our own inner approval to the world. In this act of agreement, we express our human freedom, the freedom of taking a position towards something. *The consequence of this is a life of inner agreement to that which is.*

This agreement does not refer to an unquestioned surrender or to the relinquishment of what belongs to the self. It is, in a much humbler way, an acceptance of what lies in front of us. Such acceptance does not imply that we consider everything that exists great. For one individual it may simply imply saying, "Yes, even this difficulty belongs to my life." Or, "Yes, even these burdening experiences of my story, perhaps of my childhood, belong to my life." This is of course easier when one is not in danger anymore.

If one has accepted that which exists, the next question is, what do I do with this situation? How do I want to deal with it? The ability to answer these questions means we do not have to live in a permanent opposition to life. Accepting or saying *yes* to that which exists, does not occur at only one point in a person's life, but is, rather, a constant challenge and one that exasperates people to varying degrees.

3. **"Happiness is the complicated interaction between what we have and what we want"** (Ernst, 1997, p. 23).

    Happiness develops from the successful balance between our will and our possibilities, a balance that must be achieved predominantly in the present! Our will essentially runs ahead a little. This is how the future is formed. It waits for us; we experience surprises. Life becomes suspenseful. For example, perhaps you want to go on a vacation in the coming days or weeks. You imagine what the country, the city, or the countryside will be like. Or you consider how to best invest your leisure time. And so you begin to become excited about the future, about the trip. Of course it is wise if your thoughts, the thoughts that fascinate and challenge you, remain in the field of realistic possibilities. It is here that you find the overlapping area between what is possible and what you want. In existential analysis we therefore state that *the will must always stay bound to the possibilities that a person actually has*, otherwise that person's will becomes an unrealistic wish. In this example, perhaps you never get to the country that you wanted to visit because you have already spent your money. Or perhaps you cannot enjoy the free time you have because you are consumed with thoughts about unfinished business or things that have to be completed.

Within this interaction of what we have and what we want, there must be a healthy realism. Happiness needs a realistic estimate about personal goals and possibilities. *The happy person is able to lower his or her expectations or, if necessary, intensify his or her efforts.* Such a person realises which strategy is best in each case.

Consider the following: Either we have the ability to lower our expectations by realising that a vacation is just not in the cards at the moment because we lack the money, or we intensify our efforts by saving our money efficiently and foregoing certain things in order to travel. Whatever the case, there is no single rule that is applicable to everyone. Everyone decides for themselves how important or how valuable something is to them and each person decides what he or she is willing to do or to sacrifice on account of this. There are people who always complain and lament about what they do not have at the moment. These people remain in a condition of surrender. They perceive themselves as victims and are not willing to either lower their expectations or to activate their efforts. They always compare themselves to others with respect to their own deficits. It would be much more productive for them to compare themselves to others in a positive way.

Gaining a healthy realism between what we have and what we want (compare Ernst, 1997, p. 24) results (or is reflected) in a mixture of short-term and long-term interests, in short-term and long-term wishes and life goals. The balance between small moments of happiness in one's daily life (music, fellowship, bodily enjoyments) and long-term goals must be appropriate, otherwise we forget to live in the here and now (We would then only be living in order to achieve our big goal).

4. **Ideal circumstances for happiness have an astoundingly small influence on its realisation.**

This commonly held view is confirmed through scientific analyses in the field of happiness. Let us take the example of money and fame: it may be comforting to possess sufficient money, but money does not automatically lead to happiness. It is worth noting that the law of decreasing usefulness applies here. As soon as certain minimum needs are satisfied, any further contribution tends to result in lesser emotional profit. The same is true of physical beauty, intelligence, and even of health. The reason for this is that we grow accustomed to a certain condition and then believe it to be normal.

More importantly, people can be happy despite having experienced great tragedy. Research on happiness addresses the *adaptability of the psyche* and how it regulates itself according to the objective circumstances of life (compare Ernst, 1997, p. 22). In existential analysis we believe that each person has the ability to take a position towards the objective circumstances of his or her life. This is the reason why people often say, money doesn't make you happy. Because logotherapy is a specialised field within existential analysis, a significant part of it deals with the demanding question, how are people able to sensually experience life in the face of unalterable strokes of cruel fate? At this point we have dealt with the possibility of realising attitudinal values. In the following section I want to briefly elaborate on several more important thoughts.

5. **Work is a source of happiness.**
   The reason for this is that we can realise creative values in work. On the other hand, leisure is often a source of stress, boredom, and disappointed expectations. This is because leisure time may not be experienced as supported by personally significant values. In times of leisure the person must determine the values for themselves while in work this is done for them. If these values are not personally significant or if their source is merely a wishful attitude, then existential frustration is the consequence.

6. **Happy people are active.**
   They are fulfilled doing what they do. By being active, a certain degree of self-forgetfulness is achieved. In the research conducted on happiness, this state is described as "flow-state" (Csikszentmihalyi, 1987, pp. 58–59). Psychological and physical abilities are tested to the maximum. A challenge that is too low leads to boredom; a challenge that is too intense causes fear and frustration. But when a person succeeds in handling a demanding task, the result is a higher feeling of self-worth and this, in turn, leads to happiness. This is especially so when people not only reach the peak of their abilities but when they attempt to go beyond this level. The adjective

"demanding" does not refer in this context to the degree of general performance but, rather, it is to be understood in a completely individualistic sense, as something that poses a challenge to the individual person. This activity is characterised by intentionality; it is not a form of blind activism, nor a performance-oriented fulfilment of duty. Manes Sperber expressed it thus: "Happiness is a reward for overcoming" (compare in Ernst, 1997, p. 23).

An important aspect of self-transcendence is experienced in this flow-state: the individual's connection to something other than him or herself. In such a case, people experience themselves as connected to the world or to other people in the world. And they do this through the fulfilment they find in the activity. The experience of separation between people and their surroundings is minimal or slight. These people experience a paradox: even though they experience self-forgetfulness, they experience simultaneously a high degree of self-assurance (compare also Kast, 1997, p. 53). Frankl considers this a main characteristic of self-transcendence: people find something while they are not devoted to themselves.

7. **Happy people are able to let go and relax.**
   This is because they have understand and have experienced, how it feels to be in tension and then to feel free, easy, wide, in relaxation. For them it is important to seek relaxation after tension. It is good to develop the ability for contemplation and day-dreaming. In existential analysis we call this the realisation of experiential values.

8. **"Happy people find and promote many small occasions to feel good and to be joyful about something—they do this continuously"** (Ernst, 1997, p. 23).
   When was the last time, for example, you cooked something for yourself and your partner simply because it was nice to be together? As the German saying states, if I want to have a party, I must also invite people. Opportunities exist but "unless you do something good, there is no good."[1]

   For people who are happy, happiness is not a clear goal, but an attitude. That is why psychologists speak of the *character mode of happiness* (in contrast to the condition mode of happiness, like a thrill, for example). Happiness is a way of living in the world and seeing the many possibilities for happiness that lie along the way. We see the reference to Frankl once again: a happy person does not aspire towards happiness because this is not even possible.

Happiness needs a reason in order to come into effect. One could say that only those who concentrate on something other than their happiness are in fact happy. As soon as we ask if we are happy, we stop being happy. I cannot desire, for example, the experience of joy. Joy requires a reason in order to be experienced. It is similar to the question of meaning: we do not ask whether an experience is meaningful. Again, if we ask the question, we have already lost the meaning.

Happy people experience those sides of life that bring joy and fulfilment. Further, they take these feelings with them and do not make them the goal of their life. Happiness incorporates our activities and subsequent experiences. People who are happy internalise successful, joyful, and inspiring experiences. Otherwise these experiences of happiness would remain superficial. The person who internalises happiness wins a certain attitude: she becomes a lucky duck! It seems to me that such attitudes also include the experience of deep thankfulness, because a person knows that she has no right to this happiness, but nevertheless, there it is!

9. **Happy people invest a lot of time and energy in relationships with people who are important to them.**
   They assume that other people value and like them. Further, such people have elevated emotions that strive towards connectedness. Such people celebrate with friends and not alone.

   The substantial cause of happiness, the golden key to unlocking it, has not yet been mentioned, but this key opens up the deepest experience of happiness for us:

10. **Happy people have the inner knowledge that they are loved.**
    This is more than the experience of being lovable. The person who has the experience of being loved carries it internally and is capable of accepting it. He is a lucky duck!

    Try to think back to when you were in love for the first time. You may have experienced that your existence mattered to someone or something. Children experience this when they look into the eyes of their mothers. Perhaps that is why a deep religious experience is connected to the experience of being loved.

    People who know that they are loved also know about the power of their love and, indeed, the ability to love and the possibility of loving others. Such people can, with self-respect, stay connected to this ability even when their love is not returned.

Conclusive remarks

Let me conclude with a few contemplative words. Happiness cannot be forced. It requires the ability to relax. This contradicts the attitude that sees happiness as the result of fast-living and the satisfaction of needs. Happiness has much more to do with the ability to refrain, to wait, and to not constantly see oneself as the centre of the world, instead trusting that we are able to deal with disappointments and pain because in the long run love is stronger than hate and because life is in fact good to us.

Note

1. Direct tranlation of German saying: *Es gibt nichts Gutes. außer man tut es.*

References

Csikszentmihalyi, M. (1987). *Das Flow-Erlebnis: Jenseits von Angst und Lange-weile.* Stuttgart: Klett-Cotta.
Ernst, H. (1997). Wer ist glücklich? *Psychologie Heute 24*: 20–27.
Frankl, V. (1982). *Der Wille zum Sinn.* Bern; Stuttgart; Wien: Huber, 20f.
Frankl, V. (1984). *Der leidende Mensch: Anthropologische Grundlagen der Psyc-hotherapie.* Bern; Stuttgart; Toronto: Huber.
Frankl, V. (1985). *Ärztliche Seelsorge: Grundlagen der Logotherapie und Existenz-analyse.* Frankfurt/Main: Fischer, 52f.
Kast, V. (1997). *Freude, Inspiration, Hoffnung.* München: DTV.

CHAPTER THREE

Spirituality in psychotherapy? The relationship of immanence and transcendence in existential analysis

Alfried Längle

Psychotherapy is generally understood as the treatment of psychological blocks, problems, conflicts or disease. Treatment involves the mobilisation of both psychological and spiritual forces. While psychotherapy consists of specific methods and techniques, the question arises of whether spirituality can have an appropriate place in therapy at all. The relationship between psychotherapy and religion or spirituality is therefore not usually dealt with in clinical psychotherapy. Clinical psychotherapy generally keeps a distance from what it commonly refers to as its "competitor" or "predecessor": religious or pastoral care. The references to transcendence and the (often unconscious and implicit) spiritual foundations and axioms of psychotherapy are seldom discussed. The pursuit of spirituality may in fact become a crucial issue facing psychotherapy because the differences of the psychotherapeutic methods are, to a great extent, founded on implicit spiritual references but remain, for the most part, hidden.

Introduction

A person who consults a psychotherapist is looking for a *specific offer*: he or she wants a problem solved, wants to be able to handle certain conflicts or even to be healed from psychological and psychosomatic states of suffering.

People who are in *psychological* need and, even worse, in *spiritual* despair, are consumed by their suffering to such a degree that little else concerns them beyond the necessary dealing with their existence—with the ground of their Dasein and the means by which they might handle life sufficiently in order to make it endurable and perhaps even discover some small purpose to it. Psychological and spiritual suffering is the *most unbearable form of suffering*. It takes hold of people at the core or centre of their being themselves, making it *imperative* to change something within in order to get rid of it.

In the oppression of suffering people experience something new: they feel virtually *cracked open* for a certain time, open to everything that could possibly help. This does not necessarily imply that they possess a high degree of spirituality, since by the imperative-existential character of suffering the human being is correctly and purposefully very *pragmatic*: open to everything—provided it helps.

It is only when the possibility for change seems unavailable or impossible that a person may try to understand the *foundation* of his suffering. At this point, a person may be prepared to revise his *attitude* towards life: he begins to sum up its value, to give up, let go, sink into resignation, or, in the best-case scenario, to discover a new and deeper relationship with his own existence. This is why psychological-spiritual suffering in particular can *break open* or *deepen* a person. Psychological-spiritual suffering is itself existential.

When a person consulting a psychotherapist is looking for the same *pragmatic help* as an asthmatic or cardiac patient does from the medical doctor, then it is questionable whether spirituality or even religion should play any role at all. Does psychotherapy, as a healing profession, allow for the spiritual dimension? Or is the spiritual dimension, on the contrary, much more entangled than we are aware? Do spiritual or religious psychotherapists make better "helpers"? Is psychotherapy in the end a spiritual or religious matter?

In addition to these questions, others begin to surface: Is it *appropriate* to implement this specific dimension into the framework of psychotherapy? Could such implementation run the risk of illegitimately imposing a world view—or even being an abuse of the patient's religious needs by a discipline unable to provide the healing that is promised and sold? (Cf. also Scharfetter, 1999)

Conversely, again it has to be asked, might this not lead to a splitting and fractioning of the unity and totality of the human being if the spiritual or religious dimensions of a patient are ignored, even when it is brought in not explicitly but only implicitly? Would existence not be shortened to such an extent that a human being would lose the fruitful tension that brings him out of the purely physical conditioning and vital factuality; that which brings him into the wakened, open, and active dialogue with himself and the world; that forms the basis for all psychic health and successful personhood of the human being?

What can psychotherapy do?

Psychotherapy is a scientifically based and empirically verified approach to helping people with psychological, psychosomatic, and social problems or suffering. It does this through psychological means (e.g., Kriz, 2001; Strotzka, 1984; Stumm & Wirth, 1994; Stumm, 2000; § 1 of the Austrian law of psychotherapy). The transmission of spiritual issues is hence neither the aim nor duty of psychotherapy, and clearly differs from any religiously based care or help.

There have been numerous analyses on the effectiveness of psychotherapy and what it can actually achieve (e.g., Eckert, 1996; Eckert et al., 1996; Frank, 1981; Grawe et al., 1994; Garfield & Bergin, 1986; Lang, 1990). What psychotherapy must be able to do, by definition, is provide help for a better dealing with psychological problems and suffering. At this point there has to be made a *distinction with pastoral care and religion*, but also with sects and ideologies. Psychotherapy is not a prophetic promise or a path to salvation that frees people from the painful and tragic conditions of existence. Psychotherapy does not represent a promise of salvation. It is, to state it rather harshly, only concerned with statistical probabilities on psychological improvement. It does not make references to transcendence but, rather, to methodologies and subjective resources. It does not promise life after death but demands hard work, which at times can be painful. Psychotherapy, to use a traditional differentiation, cannot offer *salvation* but can stimulate *healing* (Frankl, 1959, p. 704). It has neither the ability nor the authority to hand out salvation. Any such attempt, whether explicit or implicit, is to be seen as a spiritual abuse of the patient's hopes. Such an attempt twists the patients' religious quests and strivings and may take advantage of them. Psychotherapy cannot, and should not, attempt to replace religion. It cannot measure up to the quality of religious predications and instructions. And besides, no psychotherapeutic method has received a divine call for healing. Psychotherapy is a craft created by humans. As such, it may open up a way for people, but it cannot promise a goal (see also Scharfetter, 1999).

Another vision of psychotherapy that lets behind the ground of factuality must be demystified in order not to cause damage. Psychotherapy can only help as much as a patient is willing to contribute. This includes the patient's resources and the extent to which the patient is capable of experiencing, feeling, and living through his problems during therapy (Grawe, 1995; Grawe et al., 1994). The indication of psychotherapy is given and limited by its approach and the instruments used.

In this context stands the specific approach of existential–analytical work. Since existential analysis works explicitly and practically with the personal-spiritual dimension of the patient, it is appropriate to deal with a patient's implicit relationship to spirituality. The application of this dimension leads to the existential-analytical goal: to help people to live and act with *inner consent*. The focus on the inner consent connects with authenticity, brings ashore what is truly personal. To live and behave authentically means the realisation of the *freedom* of the person, making it present through a continuously felt inner "yes" that accompanies our actions (Längle, 2002).

What is existence?—The four constitutive fields of existence

One could say briefly that existence is the *realisation of being a person*. Viktor Frankl (1981) indicated "self-distancing" and "self-transcendence" as the anthropological preconditions for this realisation, which enable us to respond to the demands of the world. In order to come to existence, we do need, on the one hand, a certain distance to ourselves; this, on the other hand, opens us up to be able to transcend ourselves in order that we can devote oureselvesto what the world both demands and offers. Dialogical openness and dialogical interaction with both the inner and outer worlds is the medium through which existence is lived out and meaning is discovered. Frankl saw meaning as the third constitutive element of existence, taking meaning as "the call of the present". This refers to what a person believes "ought to be done" under the circumstances in a given moment. Thus human beings are answering the questions of life. Dialogical openness and *dialogical exchange* with the inner and outer worlds are the media through which existence comes to its fulfilment.

The personal basis for existence is seen in EA in the *decidedness* of the individual, that is, in the actualisation of the free will that is manifesting itself in a life with *inner consent*, as exposed above (this position distinguishes EA from the metaphysical schools of psychotherapy, like Frankl's Logotherapy, as Espinosa set out in 1998).

A characteristic of existence is that everything a person perceives and lives through is viewed as a demand placed on him (Frankl, 1984, 1987). These experiences challenge us to take a personal position.

All facts that confront humankind can be grouped into four categories, which correspond to the already mentioned horizons:

- the *world* and its conditions and possibilities;
- one's own *life*, the nature of the human in its entire vitality;
- one's own *personhood*, a distinguishable self;
- the *future* and its demand to act, the active integration of the person into the contexts in which she both lives and which she creates.[1]

> These are the four fundamental dimensions that constitute existence: the ontological, vital-axiological, ethical, and practical dimensions. Together they encompass existence sufficiently to provide the ability to live a fulfilling existence (Längle, 1992a, 1994c, 1997a, 1997b, 1998).
>
> In existential analysis, references to the world, to life, to self, and to the future are the four basic categories of existence. If these four can be lived out adequately and if their depth can be felt, they represent the *basic conditions for a fulfilled existence*. These categories constantly permeate every area of our lives (e.g., Längle, 1992b). A person is constantly trying to keep these four conditions in balance, to fulfil them as best she can, to correspond to them, and to respond to them. This sense of response is the reason why the four conditions of existence also represent the four existential motivations (cf. Längle, 1992a, 1998, 2002). The motivations are:

1. The motivation for *physical* survival and spiritually coping with existence. This means *to be able to be*.
2. The motivation to possess a *psychological* lust for life. The motivation to experience values. This means *a person likes to live*.

3. The motivation for *personal* authenticity and justice. This means *a person is allowed to be as she is.*
4. The motivation towards *existential* meaning and the development of values. This corresponds to *the way a person should act.*

If people possess these four characteristics, they *"can* be", they *"like* to live", they "are *allowed* to be as they are", and they "know what *should* be done". A real, personal, and existential "will" is then possible.

Transcendential references within existential analysis

These basic conditions for a fulfilled existence constitute the structural model of contemporary existential analysis. The model serves as a basis for diagnostics, therapy, and the theory of diseases (e.g., Längle, 1992a, 2002). At the foundation of this model we discover that all four "basic conditions for a fulfilled existence" cross over into a *transcendental relationship.* This relationship can be felt intuitively in a psychological-subjective manner. Jaspers accurately stated, "The being remains *unclosed* to us; from all sides it pulls us into the limitless" (1974, p. 13). Further, "The Encompassing is what always only *announces itself*—in the factual present and within the horizons—but it *never* becomes *the object* itself. This entity does not appear itself, but through it everything else appears. At the same time it is not only that by which everything is as it directly seems to be, but it also makes and keeps the objects transparent" (ibid., p. 14). The value of this consciousness of vastness is that the Encompassing "keeps *one's own possibility* awake". The act of "thinking of the Encompassing while widening the space opens up the soul to the perception of the origin" (ibid., p. 23).[2]

Establishing this intuitive, scenting reference forms a widening-up and a deepening of the work of existential analysis. Only then are the prerequisites of our inner and outer dialogues firmly *grounded* with regard to the world, to life, to self, and to the future. To be in open inter-action with these four dimensions is the foundation of psychological health and existential fulfilment.

All psychotherapies attempt to take into account the whole human being. In order to do this, psychotherapy has to acknowledge other disciplines and this includes spirituality. Without this acknowledgement, psychotherapy would not, in fact, be therapy but merely the practice of psycho-technique. Let us then take a closer look at the references that existential analysis has to spirituality. Let us examine where the effectiveness of existential analysis ends and where it borders the transcendent.

The first fundamental condition of existence: can I be?

The first condition is grounded in the simple fact of being in the world. This fact confronts us with the fundamental question of existence: "I am—can I be?" In other words, can I literally settle into "my world" under these conditions and with these possibilities? In order to do this, a person needs protection, space, and support. If these are lacking, the person feels restless, insecure, and anxious (Längle, 1996). When we experience protection, space, and support, however, we receive trust in the world and in ourselves. This trust may possibly even extend to a God. An amalgamation of these experiences of trust results in the fundamental trust, the ultimate trust in what we sense as the foundational support in our lives.

Let us take a closer look at the deep structure of this dimension, the fundamental trust. When we view it existentially, we are confronted with questions like this: If everything I put my trust in suddenly came undone—my relationships, my profession, or health, for example—what kind of support would I still have? Would there still be something I would experience as "trust", a foundational or basic trust that would accompany me through life and even into death? Or would there be nothing left? Would I feel as though I were in a "free fall"? On what is my trust ultimately founded upon? Is it:

- on myself;
- on other people;
- on something greater, on something which is the basis for everything else (like structures)?

A sense or sensing of being completely supported can be called the "ground of being": the feeling that there is something on which I can trust, even in the case of death. The ground of being is the psychological experience of being kept and held in any circumstance. It does not matter if the ground of being is a specific being or nothing at all (either something goes on after death or there is nothing—when sensing the ground of being, the feeling of being kept and supported is essential).

If we give our consent to this ultimate felt being, the fundamental trust emerges. Fundamental trust means that we have accepted the being as a whole. We feel we belong and that we are kept up. This is the *ontological basic experience*. This is the experience that, "There is always something that gives me support and that is bigger than I am"—a world, an order, a cosmos, a nothing at all, a god. The ground of being conveys the feeling, "If my fear and its cause were to continue, I could still accept it, even if it leads to death. I can do this because I feel ultimately kept and supported." To experience the ground of being leads to the attitude of being able to let things be (*Gelassenheit*), of being at ease, of being laid back. It is the precondition for the development of fundamental trust.

This deep and foundational experience of being supported allows a person to respond with a complete "yes" to the world and its conditions—that is, to accept the facts and conditions of our lives and to live in the midst of them, to be able to bear what is difficult.

The ground of being is like the ground in which trees have their roots (an idea originally posited by Heidegger in 1979). We cannot grasp the ground of being completely, but only repeatedly make references to it. We can only touch it from the outside and suck up its nutrients like roots from the ground and transport them from the depth to a certain height, to the "glade of being".

The ground of being can be grasped psychologically. It can be approached experientially. Yet it is also possible to reflect upon it philosophically, or describe it in a theological or religious manner. Further, it plays a bearing role in the experience of faith.

The second fundamental condition of existence: liking to live

Life establishes itself when the human being finds sufficient room in the world. It is not enough to simply be there; this being should also be *good*. Existence is more than mere fact or mechanics. Existence is lived and suffered. To live means to cry and to laugh, to feel joy and pain, to go through pleasant and unpleasant experiences, to experience both good and bad luck, and to be confronted with what is of value and what might be worthless. But it is not decided automatically that we agree with this kind of life and suffering.

In this second condition of existence we are confronted with the fundamental question of life: "I am alive—but do I like to live?" Is it a *good* thing to be here? It is not only the strains and sufferings of life that steal our joy of life; sometimes the routines of daily life and our inattentiveness when it comes to making the right choices can make life seem rather stale. In order to enjoy and literally *like* living, we again need three things: relationships, time, and closeness. The lack of closeness, time, and relationships generates a longing, an experience of coldness, and, eventually, depression. The experience of closeness, time, and relationships is conversely accompanied by a resonance with the world and oneself in which we feel the depth of life. These experiences make up the fundamental value of existence. They are both the deepest feelings we have for the value of existence, and experiences of being touched by life. This fundamental value accompanies every form of experience. It colours our emotions and affects and becomes the template for what feels "valuable" to us.

In the depth of this turning towards, appears the ultimate and deep experience of being touched by life, which we encounter in the everyday forms of being touched—in relationships, in music, and in all forms of feelings in our everyday lives. Allowing ourselves to be deeply touched by life also includes experiences of suffering and pain. This being touched confronts us with the fundamental question of life: What is it like for me personally to live and to exist? How does this life feel when I look at all the years that have passed and those yet to come? When I take into account all the hurt and pain, the suffering, the violence, the joy and bliss? When I take notice of my own beating heart, what is the "sound" like within me? What comes to the surface when I feel my life this way?

It is important to *open* ourselves to this inner motion. We need to be open to this most personal, inner relationship and to be touched by the being. When we truly *feel* our lives, we must be open and non-judgemental towards that which surfaces. This inner experience of life makes it possible to sense the "value of life itself", to see how it shows up in our own biographies (and by empathising also in the biographies and destinies of other people as well). In all the numerous individual experiences we have, life tells us about its value. It invites us to commit ourselves to it (what lacks in burnout—Längle, 1997c).

What appears here in the depth of our sensing is an inkling of the value which has life itself. Much like the depth of "being" which lead us to the ground of being, we now come to the "fundamental value" of existence. This is the foundational value at the root of any value experience. When we experience the value of life, we experience something that transcens us. We realise that experiencing something of value does not rely solely on us and is not created by us but comes towards us, is received by us. We discover it, astonished perhaps, amazed, painfully touched, or silenced, grateful.

The third fundamental condition of existence: am I allowed to be?

Despite the fact that each person is connected to life and other people, everyone perceives himself or herself to be *his or her* own person, as being uniquely different. Uniqueness makes us an "I". It is what separates us from everyone else.

This sense of uniqueness confronts us with the *fundamental question of being a person (personhood)*: "I am myself—am I allowed to be this way?" Do I have the right to be as I am and to act the way I do? These questions reside at the level of identification, of discovering the self, and of ethics. People need attention, justification, and appreciation to manage this level. People who lack these experience loneliness. They hide behind shame and hysteria may develop. If, however, people possess these three conditions, they are capable of reaching authenticity, comfort, and self-respect. The sum of these experiences constitutes self-worth and personhood, the deepest value of the ego.

In this depth, the human being is confronted with the fact that they "cannot be grasped" entirely: Who is this "I"? How can this "I" be fixated? We approach the basis of our "ego" when we listen to the voice within us that calls us emotionally. "It" speaks inside of me—and it speaks to "me". This inner "sound" is accompanied by the feeling that I am being meant.

When the ego takes up this "it"—that is, that which starts speaking within the person—the human being becomes authentic. Personhood essentially means to attend oneself, to encounter oneself as one who is confided to oneself. The "place" of encounter between the person and oneself (of this "I and myself"), where the person meets herself, is the place of her *intimacy*. It is the "place of salience" of the person. To be a person ultimately means to be continuously gifted from the side of oneself.

Once again, we are confronted with the *mystery* of existence, confronted with something we are unable to fully grasp yet intimately connected to. Nothing is closer to us than our most inner being, our identity, and our ego. Yet we experience this deep inside as something that flows towards us and which escapes our control and full knowledge, but which appears within us, in our own intimacy. We experience it as something we can refer to. Jaspers describes it as follows:

> We are not free on account of ourselves. But in our freedom we are given to ourselves. And we do not know by whom or from where. We are not on account of ourselves. This is the way things are: we cannot want our will. We cannot plan who we are in our freedom. But the reality is that the origin or starting point of all our planning and of our will is that through which we are given to ourselves ... Just like the fact that we have not created ourselves, so this freedom does not exist on account of us, but it is a gift to us ... How does this come about? -Obviously this gift is not of this world. (1984, p. 48)

The fourth fundamental condition of existence: the way a person should act

If a person is able to be, to enjoy and like his life, to discover his unique self in the world, he requires only one more thing in order to achieve fulfilment: a relation to the constant change, to the becoming and developing that provides the background or horizon of where he is. It is not enough to simply be and to have found or discovered ourselves. We want to transcend our immediate situation; we want to rise above ourselves and discover *what* life and existence is all about. Each human being is directed towards transcending himself and being merged with something else. This makes our days! We want to become fruitful. Otherwise it would be as if we lived in a house in which nobody comes to see us.

Thus the transitory nature of our being-there puts before us the question of the meaning of our existence: *"I am here—for what good?"* To answer this, we need three things: a field of activity, a structural connection, and a value in the future. If these are lacking, the consequences are emptiness, frustration, and even despair, which is often accompanied by addiction. If we possess these three things, we have the ability to commit ourselves and to act wholly, eventually to a form of religiosity. The sum of these experiences makes up the *meaning of life* and culminates in a fulfilled existence.

It is not enough though to have a field of activity, to know oneself being in a context and to have values in the future wanting to be achieved. We also need a *phenomenological attitude*. This attitude is the existential entry point to existence: the position of openness that enables situations to *speak to us* (Frankl, 1987; Längle, 1984). "What does this moment demand of me and to what shall I reply?" Since existence is dialogical, it is not enough to simply ask what I can expect from life, but also what life expects *of me*. What does a situation expect *of me*? What can and should *I* do now, for other people as for myself? My active part in creating this position of openness is to accommodate the situation. I need to examine and assess whether my actions are good for others, for myself, for the future, and for the world in which I stand. And so my existence is fulfilling when I *act* this way.

Viktor Frankl described meaning as "an actual possibility before the background of reality" (1987, p. 315). This definition should be expanded slightly: meaning is "the most *valuable* possibility present in the situation". Further, meaning is both existential and ontological. Existential meaning is that which is possible, most valuable, and interesting to *me* in light of the facts and realities that are present. Existential meaning is what the present situation or circumstance both requires and demands of me. We have an inner sense, though, that enables us to reduce the complexity of life's demands and requests and make tasks both liveable and manageable. Besides existential meaning, existential analysis addresses an ontological meaning. This is meaning of the totality in which a human being stands. The meaning of the whole does not depend upon a single person. It is the philosophical and religious meaning, the meaning of the creator that I may approach by intuition and belief (on the differentiation between existential and ontological meaning: see Längle, 1994b, 1995). In this fourth dimension we encounter once again the encompassing, the mystery of life, and faith. Spirituality becomes indispensable in the ontological quest for meaning. The sensing strives to more knowledge and recognition, to religious formulation and denomination.

Spirituality from an existential analytical perspective

Let us turn, in conclusion, to a *reflection* on the relationship of existential analysis and spirituality. We could summarise the results as follows:

1. **The anthropological definition: human beings are spiritual-mental beings.**

   A human being is by nature a spiritual being in the sense of rising above matter and the vitality of nature. We have the capacity to act and to perceive, to take positions, and to become effective in action. This capacity is "spiritual" in the sense that "spirit" and "matter" are in contrast to each other. But "spiritual" is not used in the sense of inspiration from the Holy Spirit.

2. **The existential definition: spirituality as the basis of existence.**

   Human beings (persons) depend on a mental-spiritual capturing of the facts and givens in order to live out our lives and interact with the world, dealing with it according to our (spiritual) essence. Human beings' fundamental relatedness (to others as to themselves) attests to the "spiritual disposition" within humankind. This existential spirituality is the human ability to analyse and penetrate a given circumstance in order to understand it—what the "givens" "give". This uniquely human predisposition is a phenomenological openness and an ability to let ourselves be touched by life in order to push through to the "logos" of a given moment. To what has been understood (noema) the human being develops an attitude, a mood (which can be seen as an original form of attitude, a premature form of the spiritual differentiation).

   However, penetrating the depth and potential of human existence is always covered by the day-to-day routines of life. It belongs to the essence of existence being constantly distracted from this depth, where we potentially lose ourselves. Not surprisingly, the ability to "hear the sound within", and subsequently orient and position ourselves towards that sound, remains most often unconscious. We remain spiritual beings, however, and this can be seen in the spontaneity in which we live our lives, in the vast range of our moods and emotions, and in our ability to make decisions.

   Spirituality, therefore, is here understood as an experiential, spiritual openness towards a greatness that exceeds the human being and his existence in all four (above mentioned) dimensions (see also Helg, 2000). It is an essential layer which humans can experience as the origin of their personhood, indeed, of existence itself, where they can experience the ultimate being kept. If these connections become conscious the human being sees himself founded in them.

Spirituality can be summed up as "experiencing the spirit in the core or centre of life".

Our spiritual foundation is the basic experience for every form of religiosity. Religiosity is barren, without flesh and blood, when it is not founded in human life. Pastoral care should not work against or without this, otherwise it would disregard the spiritual nature of humankind. True pastoral care considers the spiritual relationships embedded in our experiences, indeed life itself, and helps open us to the dimension of existential spirituality.

The personal *experience* of faith has often been neglected or even seen as inferior compared to the *transmission* of faith via the church or biblical text, for example. From an existential point of view neither of these is superior to the other when it comes to the experience of faith. They condition, supplement, and depend on each other. Therefore, they belong together.

Understanding our experiences of spirituality does not imply that we can save ourselves by our own means. Basic experiences of faith make existing possible, nothing more. They are not religious salvation. Such elements of faith, which human beings can sense, experience, and discover on their own and for which they do not depend, form the experiential basis of all religions. Religion through its different form of knowledge and the divine message, has possibilities to interpret, formulate, and express the experienced, and to place it within a larger frame of reference that includes prophecy and salvation. An individual, however, cannot fully grasp this larger frame of reference. It is, rather, experienced at the personal level as grace, an experience of acceptance that instils faith and hope despite moments of hopelessness and tragedy.

Summarising these observations, we might say that practical living relies on spirituality.[3] As persons human beings realise in their existence an openness that can never be totally closed, but which is encompassing, reaching out towards the greater and comprehensive. In this dialogical relation with the other but also with oneself—it cannot be separated any more within the depth of this relation— a specific faith has its origin which can be considered as an inevitable "existential faith" before any religious form of belief has developed. This means it starts before the active religious search begins and before this kind of being is more accurately defined.

This "existential faith transmits a deep experience and feeling of being at home, of belonging, and even more. It gives a person—to iterate it at the end once more—a deep sense of being fundamentally *supported and kept*, of the unconditional *value* of life, of the inscrutable depth of the person and the justice beyond all calculations, and, eventually, of the deep sense of being in an all-encompassing context in which we make the effort to find a meaning in each act throughout our entire life.

Notes

1. Karl Jaspers (1965) seems to have a similar approach. In his article "On my philosophy" (first published in *Logos*, 1941, volume 24) he writes: "In every aspect of his being, a human is referred to an other, as existing (Dasein) to his world, as consciousness generally to objects, as spirit to the idea of the respective whole, as existence to transcendence" (1965, p. 19) Although this passage mainly describes the development of the whole person through the reference to other things, it is interesting to see that Jaspers differentiates four different aspects of being to which different contents are assigned. The same figure of thought underlies the concept of fundamental motivations. There is, however, a difference in categorisation; thus they are only distantly related.

2. For Jaspers, the experiences of suffering, guilt, death, struggle, and chance are inevitable, immutable basic situations of life (Dasein). Therefore, he calls them *"boundary situations"* (Jaspers, 1986, p. 20f). These situations radically shake up the existence of the subject as such, awakening them to existence (Jaspers, 1956, vol. I, p. 56). The only meaningful reaction to boundary situations is not to try to overcome them, but to attempt to confront them openly, in order to make existence possible within us. "Experiencing boundary situations and existing (Existenz) is the same thing" (1956, vol. II, p. 204).

    The in-depth concept of fundamental motivations could be described as a boundary experience. But this experience of depth does not have the typically tragic character of existential philosophy. "Boundary experiences" in the fundamental existential motivations also form the foundation of existence, as Jaspers describes it for boundary situations. I assume that the experience of boundary situations leads to those contents which have been described in the fundamental motivations. The experience, thereby, leads to the awakening of the existence.

3. Karl Jaspers states it similarly: "Existence is the being oneself that relates and acts to itself and, thereby, to the transcendent. It knows itself to be a

gift from the transcendent and also knows that the self is founded upon it" (1975, p. 17). Or, in a religious terminology: "God is for me to that degree as I properly exist" (1986, p. 51).

Here is another passage that seems to verify the closeness to the fundamental motivations: "It has been repeatedly demonstrated: For us godhood is, if it exists, only in such a way as he appears to us in the world, as he speaks to us through the language of people and the world ... Only in those ways which are understandable to humans the godhood comes into appearance" (Jaspers, 1965, pp. 20–21).

Or consider this passage: A human "owes himself to himself. Yet at the same time he does not know how he was capable of this. He sees the limits of his freedom: he knows that he only has a will when he is free. But he cannot have freedom through his will. On account of this, he knows that his self is a gift. But he does not know, experience or feel through some trustworthy experience that there is another power to thank for his self. He knows that his self was given to him as a present, but he does not know its origin—a being given to oneself that has the character that it owes in it to itself, full of tension, openness and demanding good will" (Jaspers, 1952, p. 42).

References

Bauer, E. (2000). Wenn die Sinnhaftigkeit des Sinns in Frage steht. *Existenzanalyse, 17*: 4–13.

Eckert, J. (1996). Schulenübergreifende Aspekte der Psychotherapie. In: Ch. Reimer, J. Eckert, M. Hauzinger, & E. Wilke (Eds.), *Psychotherapie: Ein Lehrbuch für Ärzte und Psychologen* (pp. 324–329). Berlin: Springer.

Eckert, J., Hauzinger, M., Reimer, Ch., & Wilke, E. (1996). Grenzen der Psychotherapie. In: Ch. Reimer, J. Eckert, M. Hauzinger, & E. Wilke (Eds.), *Psychotherapie: Ein Lehrbuch für Ärzte und Psychologen* (pp. 525–535). Berlin: Springer.

Espinosa, N. (1998). Zur Aufgabe der Logotherapie und Existenzanalyse im nachmetaphysischen Zeitalter. *Existenzanalyse, 15*: 4–12.

Frank, J. D. (1981). *Die Heiler: Wirkweisen psychotherapeutischer Beeinflussung: Vom Schamanismus bis zu den modernen Therapien*. Stuttgart: Klett-Cotta.

Frankl, V. (1959). Grundriß der Existenzanalyse und Logotherapie. In: V. Frankl, V. v. Gebsattel, & J. H. Schultz (Eds.), *Handbuch der Neurosenlehre und Psychotherapie* (Bd. III, pp. 663–736). München/Wien: Urban & Schwarzenberg.

Frankl, V. (1984). *Der leidende Mensch: Anthropologische Grundlagen der Psychotherapie*. Bern: Huber.

SPIRITUALITY IN PSYCHOTHERAPY? 51

(1997) *Süchtig sein: Entstehung, Formen und Behandlung von Abhängigkeiten* (pp. 13–33). Wien: Facultas.

Längle, A. (1997b). Modell einer existenzanalytischen Gruppentherapie für die Suchtbehandlung. In: A. Längle & Ch. Probst (Eds.) (1997) *Süchtig sein: Entstehung, Formen und Behandlung von Abhängigkeiten* (pp. 149–169). Wien: Facultas.

Längle, A. (1997c). Burnout—Existentielle Bedeutung und Möglichkeiten der Prävention. *Existenzanalyse, 14*: 11–19.

Längle, A. (1998.) Lebenssinn und Psychofrust—zur existentiellen Indikation von Psychotherapie. In: L. Riedel (Ed.), *Sinn und Unsinn der Psychotherapie* (pp. 105–124). Basel: Mandala.

Längle, A. (2002). Die Grundmotivationen menschlicher Existenz als Wirkstruktur existenzanalytischer Psychotherapie. *Fundamenta Psychiatrica, 16*: 1–8.

Scharfetter, C. (1999). *Der spirituelle Weg und seine Gefahren.* Stuttgart: Thieme.

Strotzka, H. (1984). *Psychotherapie und Tiefenpsychologie: Ein Kurzlehrbuch.* Wien: Springer, 2°.

Stumm, G. (2000). Psychotherapie. In: G. Stumm & A. Pritz (Eds.), *Wörterbuch der Psychotherapie* (pp. 569–570). Wien: Springer.

Stumm, G., & Wirth, B. (Eds.) (1994). *Psychotherapie: Schulen und Methoden.* Wien: Falter, 2°.

CHAPTER FOUR

The dimension of time as a challenge to truthful existence

Christine Wicki

Time as an essential basis for human existence

Time may be experienced as long or short. It may drag out or pass quickly. People have not given this phenomenon sufficient attention. Measurable time has been examined objectively in great detail. The subjective experience of time, however, has for the most part been disregarded, these altered perceptions often being contextualised as merely being experienced by people who lack the appropriate sense and feeling for time. In 1889 Henri Bergson was the first, to my knowledge, to raise the importance of the subjective in terms of time (Bergson, 2001). Since then, the issue of human existence and the way it is bound by time has received more attention. Our way of life is the essential factor for our conscious experience of time. This is undisputed. Human existence is always a process, a development. It takes place within time and is conditioned by time's characteristics. There is a given and set horizon for existence, for living out our lives and being-in-the-world: this horizon is called time. In general terms, time is the essential basis for human existence. It is the essential factor for change. Time is closely interwoven with every aspect of our existence. It is a phenomenon that concerns all arts and sciences and each individual person. In Heidegger's significant work *Sein und Zeit*" ("Existence and Time"), he stated:

> Time is the medium in which humankind lives out its existence primarily. In time a person develops his personality and nature. It is only in relation to time and the world that a human's nature develops a concrete form. Time has always been there. It provides the horizon for existence and being in the world. Existence develops and occurs within the dimension of time. (Heidegger, 1984, p. 54)

Further, Bollnow states: "The issue of time and its dimension directly concerns human nature" (Bollnow, 1979, p. 165).

We cannot be independent of time; it is an inseparable part of human existence. We are bound to time and each person experiences this with varying intensity. A person cannot manipulate time. We can never "turn the clocks back" or stop time. Time passes continuously throughout our lives. We cannot influence its passing, yet we can think back to certain irretrievable situations and missed opportunities. "Personal life takes place in time. This is the serious aspect of the dimension of time. A person cannot fool around with time. Either they make use of it or the opportunity passes. Time is the medium in which we either ascend or descend" (v. Gebsattel, 1958, p. 357).

The dimension of time is an expression of the finiteness of human existence. In our finiteness we are timely creatures. Time has profound meaning. Time, in fact, is somewhat intense. If we had an endless amount of time, tomorrow would be just as good as today. We would have no reason to start something, to make decisions, or to take hold of opportunities. It is only our knowledge that life is limited that moves us towards action and motivates us to give form to our life. "The pressure of finiteness makes life suspenseful. It forces a person ... to make use of their life time" (Bollnow, 1984, p. 98).

The dimensions of time and the significance for human existence

Time is often seen as a uniform and fleeting experience. It is to be understood, however, as a continuous flow of individual moments. These moments come out of the future, flow into the present, and disappear into the past. The qualitative meaning of individual moments is often not realised. It can often been the case that all that matters is the quantity of time we have, measured by the amount of experiences we have in the shortest amount of time possible.

This view is based upon a certain interpretation of time. Such a view sees time as a uniform and fleeting continuum. It is the idea that life unwinds like a thread, until it is finally cut. Everything is more or less uniform. The past is past. It does not matter anymore. The future is not here yet and therefore has no significance. Only the present is connected to *my* "present life" and is, therefore, all that matters. People believe that it is important to do as much as possible in the present and to experience life before "it" (the present) disappears into the past. This view of time causes hectic, impatient, sensationalist, and empty activity. Yet these kinds of activities inhibit a person's ability to remain in the present. At the same time, death becomes a subject not to be spoken of, since death is viewed as something terrible, threatening, and representing the end. Time is then regarded as something that approaches us from the outside and we tend to disregard the deeper purpose, the greater significance, of our present life.

It is evident that when we take a closer look at moments of time, such a view is quite limited. When we describe a present moment of time, for example, we discover that time has, in fact, a rich structure. A future moment is already contained in our individual plans, hopes, and fears. Past, present, and future cannot be understood as uniform parts of a chain. These three dimensions cannot be understood as uniform parts of a chain, but these are "the three directions human behaviour extends into and out of which the present moment is constituted". Human behaviour extends into these three directions and they make up the present moment (Bollnow, 1984, p. 106). Heidegger spoke of the three "ecstasies", or the three "dimensions" of time.

What follows is an elaboration on these three dimensions: the past, the present, and the future. These dimensions are a truth and a reality. The past and the future affect the present. All three dimensions affect humanity. In a certain sense, these dimensions form a unity because we, as existing entities, take part in all three dimensions. We must, however, be careful not to disconnect and place each dimension beside the other. These dimensions are real to the whole of existence. They are not neutral factors in human existence, nor are they experienced in the same way. Every person experiences them differently. The past can be a burden to some; in such cases the individual drags his past around with him. To another, the past might be experienced as a solid foundation, one that gives him strength. The present and future may be experienced in similar ways.

In order to experience the possible value contained in each of the three time dimensions, we must take a closer look at the relevance of time to human existence. I believe this topic can be important for the work done in therapeutic sessions.

Living life in spite of its finiteness

It is important at this juncture to make reference to the existential meaning of time dimensions and how an individual subjectively experiences them. In order to illustrate this theory, I will refer to excerpts from several therapy sessions with one of my patients. Ann (whose name has been altered for publication) is in her late twenties. I met Ann for the first time a little over a year ago. She had just been informed that she was HIV positive and she wanted to "clean up" her life. There were several issues that burdened Ann. She wanted to get rid of them but did not know how to go about it. At the beginning of our sessions her entire attention was focused on living as healthily as possible (both physically and emotionally). She wanted to triumph over her disease. As a result, she put a great deal of pressure on herself and viewed everything—people and situations—not as they really were but in light of her own health. This pressure and burden had to be loosened before further therapeutic work could begin.

Our preliminary comments on Ann's case highlight the meaning of an event in the future and its influence on present life. As stated, we are creatures of time and are therefore conscious of our finiteness. This knowledge moves and motivates us to act in the present. In fact, death and the knowledge of our finiteness is a constitutive element of our present life. Death is not merely an event that will occur at some time in the future. Bollnow writes, "The movement of life does not drive us towards death, but it causes movement in life" (Bollnow, 1984, p. 94). In this sense death, as an event in the future, becomes a moving and creative element of our present life.

My patient Ann seldom thought about her finiteness prior to her crisis. Because death had seemed so far away to her, it had not been worth thinking about. She was then abruptly confronted with death. She was confronted with the fact of her own mortality, indeed with the finiteness of her life. For the first time she had to deal with this knowledge and it contributed to a new significance and quality in her present life situation. She said, "Life has become extremely precious to me because I must now count on dying—sooner or later. I am stingy with my time. I have let go of many burdening things. I do not do all those things that everyone else does. I do not want to do stupid things just to kill time."

Knowledge of one's own death is connected to great insecurity. Only a few people know about the time of their death. Heidegger (1984) examined the effects of this and he spoke of the fearful, dizzy, and eerie feelings that accompany such knowledge. Human beings are overcome with these emotions when they think about non-existence. This has an effect upon our plans, hopes, and expectations. Because of the insecurity that arises, we are forced to find meaning for our present life. If we want to stand our ground in the face of death, we must find a fulfilling measure of meaning in the present hour. We must be concerned with the essential things in our present and immediate life. We are called upon to be resolute and live a true existence. Jaspers wrote: "Everything that remains in the face of death is accomplished existentially" (Jaspers, 1973, p. 223).

While Heidegger's thoughts are important for understanding human existence, it is not natural for us to live in fear and worry about our mortality. As human beings we believe in the possibility that we will go on living, that we will have a future, and so we plan and hope for the future. The dimension of time affects humanity in the following two-fold way: the possibility that we may die at any given time is always present;, but at the same time, we have the possibility of a future. Both of these aspects influence our present lives.

In light of this, the future plays an essential role for the present life of humankind. We are never able to say that we have accomplished our aim in life because we are always in a process of development. We are constantly becoming something else. The future is the direction for life and incorporated into the process of development. Our "life" time is focused time as it refers to the future. Our expectations and plans for the future have meaning for the present. Possibilities in the future motivate us for action. Indeed, the act of focusing on the future can characterise a person's liveliness and dynamics in the present. The kind of relationship a person has to the future is essentially meaningful for the present.

Ann had a hard time when she thought about "having a future". She did not have much faith in it. Because of this, she felt cut off from life. We talked about the possible meaning of having a future. It had always seemed very abstract to her. Although her future, measurable in years, was always present in her mind, it seemed far away. She saw no real relationship between the future and the present. She thought of the future as a vague possibility. When her life seemed empty, boring, or difficult, she hoped and trusted in what might be in the future. In such a state, she tended to romanticise the future: "Some day everything will be better. I will change completely." But in fact her future never entered the present. Ann was finally able to let go of these speculations and having a future became something very concrete for her. She now wants to seize the concrete possibilities that have yet to enter her life and let them become reality.

The importance of becoming and developing is especially real to people who are in danger of losing their future. A depressive mood, for example, is deeply connected to an altered view of the future. The future is not experienced as the possibility for development but, rather, appears eerie and threatening. The depressed person, therefore, sees no possibility for development or even life for that matter. Such a person is afraid of his own perdition. His strength and ability to achieve become weakened and eventually he feels worthless. Life loses its meaning. The potential possibilities of the future are invisible to him. As the person loses strength, hope, and assurance, feelings of guilt begin to settle in. The depressed person experiences these feelings with high intensity. Although every person feels guilty about something to a certain degree, the healthy person does not experience the pressure of guilt as intensely as the depressed person does. The healthy person sees possibilities in the future in order to deal with her guilt, while the depressed person is incapable of this because he has an altered view of the future. Guilt then "takes on an irrevocable, uncorrectable and final character. It becomes the dominating factor of depressive guilt" (v. Gebsattel, 1958, p. 366). I think the significance of having a future is quite clear.

To summarise: the future not only causes fear and worry in the present because of the reality of death and the finality of life, but the future is also the dimension for becoming and developing. It can, in fact, fill the present with strength, assurance, and hope.

The attitude towards the past

Human life, however, is not only something that is "open towards the future". The future becomes the present and then remains in our memory as the past. The significance of the past is commonly known. I therefore want to address this dimension briefly but to mention one aspect of the past that often seems to be neglected.

It is a common belief that the past "crowds" in on the present when it causes an individual to feel burdened and weighed down. The fact that the present may also affect the past is often overlooked. The present may give new meaning to the past. For example, a person may no longer be a victim of his past by virtue of creating a different meaning for his past. The past is, therefore, not merely fact, but a dimension that also demands something of us. It calls us to confront our own past for, in the end, we must take responsibility for our past and respond in the "here and now". The past must become meaningful, for, while the events of the past are an unalterable fact, how we deal with the past and what meaning it may have in the immediate depends on our current life. The way we live today can also affect the past by decreasing or increasing the significance of past events. Some meaningful aspects may be added while others may disappear.

In this sense, we must acknowledge that we carry the responsibility for our past in the "here and now". Even more so, the present also affects the past. Frankl called this the "defiant power of the human spirit": "Humanity is bound by the conditions of humanness. But the actual person also deals with his own human existence: he acts and behaves in spite of the conditions in which he is placed" (Frankl, 1975, p. 84).

In the context of our theme, this may mean that a person can "alter" his behaviour despite certain events of the past and in spite of his biography. Our present behaviour influences the significance of past events and its relevance for the present. "The factual conditioning of a human is in contrast to his facultative necessities" (Frankl, 1975, p. 85). Obviously this fact has a liberating and healing effect upon patients in therapeutic counselling.

The present: a purely actual dimension

It is hard to speak about the present. It is not a common phenomenon but an event—it is pure actuality. In this actuality a person experiences himself or herself. It is "here" where we are present. "When the future becomes the past, the world approaches us in the present ... It demands an answer, the taking of a position, a decision" (Schrey, 1947, p. 82).

The present occurs just once. It cannot be repeated. In the present a person exists in his actuality. It is here where a person immanently experiences himself. Stepping out, being-in-the-world, taking a position, for example, all are acts of true existence that take place in the present. They allow the person to find self-assurance or, more appropriately, assurance.

It is not only essential, therefore, to deal with the past in psychotherapy, but it is also the task of therapy to enable and encourage the person to become an active creator in his current life situation. From this perspective, it is possible to help people who "live almost exclusively in the past or the future". These people are in danger of losing their immanent self-assurance. They do not feel or experience themselves as acting people or creators of their world, but more often as mere spectators or even prisoners of their lives. As a result, they believe that they are at the mercy of their future.

My patient Ann now tries to feel the significance of the present and to live according to it. She receives a different feeling for life. She said,

> Only now am I truly learning who I am. Now I've finally figured out what I am good and not good at. Now I know what is important. I used to always wait for tomorrow. I thought real life took place when I found the husband of my dreams, when I had enough money to go on a big vacation, or when I had a fulfilling job. Now I know that life is also daily life, with all its heights and depths. It is strange, but now I actually feel safer and more secure than before. I do not have to hurry to catch up all the time. I do not have to wait for something all the time.

This has by no means been an exhaustive analysis on the three dimensions: the past, the present, and the future. The remarks so far were meant to draw attention to the variety of meanings for human existence.

Resolution

I would like to deal with the question of a "right" relationship to time. Bollnow wrote:

> The question of time forces itself upon a person with an incredible force. Human life must abide by the law of time. This is truly not a formal, neutral way of describing life. It is not easy to accept. It

is the expression of a deep threat which cannot be ignored. Being bound to time means that a person is transient, frail. To express it sharply: As time continuously slips by the fact that humans are bound to time makes everything vain. (Bollnow, 1987, p. 10)

But, as I have mentioned, the evanescence of time, the transience of human existence, is just one side of the dimension of time. The passing of time, the fact that existence is bound to time, also makes development and formation possible. It includes the possibility to create something new. The fact that humankind is bound to time in all situations of life calls upon every person to make decisions. Each person decides if she will let time pass aimlessly and miss a given opportunity or take hold of time and use it as an opportunity to develop her talents. Each person is responsible. Each person must decide if she will make a situation her own by exerting personal effort. This immediate effort is a meaningful and valuable act. It means that the purpose of *my* action does not depend on its achieved goal or success. Rather, the purpose depends on the immediate effort.

Heidegger spoke of "resolution" in this context. Bollnow states:

"Resolution" refers to the actual condition of human existence. The activity does not have its purpose in the goal which is to be achieved, but carries its indestructible purpose within itself. It is about the final, tense effort of human existence. This effort yanks a person out of his cloudy, drifting existence. … A person takes control of his life by exerting a certain effort. He would otherwise lose his self on account of the numerous possibilities offered to him. The purpose of this effort is not the achievement (or failure), but its purpose is the exerted, final effort. (Bollnow, 1984, pp. 108–109)

Ann struggled with this idea. On the one hand, she sensed the responsibility. She knew that things depended on her. She also sensed the freedom that might arise by living resolutely and exerting effort. She sensed the freedom of knowing that the here and now counts, that her present behaviour made all the difference. She no longer had to decide whether she should achieve success in the future or graduate from some college. This was beyond her present life. On the other hand, this was exactly what troubled her. She wondered: "If I do not finish something, if I fail at it, was it then right and good to have done it? Did it pay off?" She answered: "Yes, it was right and good, but ...". It is this "but" we shall discuss further.

Uncompromising effort, a true existence, are the essential moments of life. They are short moments which incorporate all of time. These moments are of eternal character. When we experience and live through these moments, this ascent to true existence, time has a completely different meaning. We do not see it as a threat anymore. It is not about quantity anymore. It is not about accumulating achievements or doing as much as possible. It is essential to take hold of a given situation by exerting an uncompromising effort. In this act of resolution, we achieve something. These moments can no longer be seen as merely the fleetingness of time: our actions possess meaning and value and are therefore of eternal character.

A "short moment" can incorporate time in its entirety. Here we sense the heartbeat of life. Such moments are outside of the transience of time. They have a lasting and valuable effect. The entire life of a couple, for example, may be expressed in a single glance. They experience something that is not lost to the past. The experience itself has a lasting effect. Such a moment can be experienced especially when we are in love. Søren Kierkegaard gave much attention to this thought and the depth of its meaning.

Living in time

Finally, I want to refer to a basic phenomenon of human existence. In my opinion, there is an essential connection between humankind and the dimension of time.

So far we have talked about the structure of time in human existence and the possible ways and forms of existing. But these thoughts cannot undo the insecurity of existence which is the result of being bound to time. Humankind must live with this irrevocable insecurity. While we may try to plan, to think ahead, and act, we nonetheless remain bound to this fundamental insecurity of not knowing how much time we have. We must deal with this insecurity. It is an essential part of living within the limits of time.

When someone does not evade this knowledge, then "he makes a strange experience. Rilke spoke of a turn: ... danger, all pure threat from the world—turns into protection, as you sense it [the world] entirely (or completely?)" (Bollnow, 1987, p. 90). When a person comes to the limit of her abilities, she finds a trusting relationship with the future. We all know this trusting experience as "hope".

From time to time Ann experienced insecurity and fear. She then tried to evade these experiences and thoughts. "To pretend as if …", she called it. This started a downward spiral. She tried to plan and forget about the present. She became hectic and tried to get a hold on security but simply became more and more afraid. She then came to a point where she had to admit, "I can't go on like this." She said, "When I am in such a state I cannot do anything else but hope that things will go on. And when I somehow think I will make it, everything is better again."

If a person does not want to "give up" on account of the insecurity in life, and to "become desperate, he needs some helpful power to overcome these temptations. At this point hope can do an important task" (Bollnow, 1987, p. 90).

Hope should not be understood as an attitude of bearing unpleasant things and waiting for something good. True hope gives power and assurance to a person. It motivates us for action. We must continuously work for this hope for it is not a given of human existence. In this context, Bloch refers to "learning to hope" (quoted in Bollnow, 1987, p. 80). This process of learning occurs in the here and now, in the present life situation of a person. A person learns to hope by grasping the situational possibilities and making them her own.

It is the decisive task of a person to reach for hope and constantly defend it in spite of all the temptations and desperation. Yes, this process essentially determines the experiences and sufferings of a person in regard to her timely existence.

Merleau-Ponty coined a term that accurately summarises our analysis so far. He speaks of "living in time" which means the following:

> Humanity lives in a certain physical space. He does this by settling down somewhere in this great and eerie world and makes himself at home there. He is only able to do this, in spite of all the surrounding destruction, because his final trust in the world carries him along. This is also true for time. Humanity lives in time by settling down in the present moment. He fulfils the multiple demands in this "house" of time. A person responsibly and carefully plans his present opportunities for action. With an indestructible hope he faces the open

future and, thereby, gives meaning to the present. This meaning has
value in itself and is beyond transience. (Bollnow, 1987, p. 112)

I sincerely wish we all had such living possibilities.

References

Bergson, H. (2001). *Time and Free Will: An Essay on the Immediate Data of Consciousness, 1910* (Essai sur les données immédiates de la conscience, 1889). Mineola, NY: Dover Publications.

Bollnow, O. F. (1979). *Neue Geborgenheit*. Stuttgart: Kohlhammer, 4°.

Bollnow, O. F. (1984). *Existenzphilosophie*. Stuttgart: Kohlhammer, 9°.

Bollnow, O. F. (1987). *Das Verhältnis zur Zeit*. Heidelberg: Quelle & Meyer.

Frankl, V. E. (1975). *Anthropologische Grundlagen der Psychotherapie*. Bern/Stuttgart/Wien: Hans Huber.

Heidegger, M. (1984). *Sein und Zeit*. Tübingen: Max Niemeyer, 15°.

Jaspers, K. (1973). *Philosophie II Existenzerhellung*. Berlin/Heidelberg/New York: Springer, 4°.

Schrey, H. (1947). Existenz und Offenbarung. Tübingen: Mohr.

v. Gebsattel, V. E. (1958). Die Störungen des Werdens und des Zeiterlebens im Rahmen psychiatrischer Erkrankungen. In: Roggenbau, H. (Hrsg) *Gegenwartsprobleme der psychiatrisch-neurologischen Forschung*. Stuttgart: Ferdinand Enke.

CHAPTER FIVE

Steps towards meaning: the method of grasping meaning

Helene Drexler

Martha is sitting in a cafe. She is waiting for her husband who is running an errand. She reads a couple of lines in the newspaper and places it back down on the table. She looks across the room with a lost expression on her face. Time seems to stand still. "A long *time* ago, at this time of day I used to …"

Up until a few of weeks ago Martha had worked at a doctor's office and would not have glanced at the time. She would probably have worked until late in the evening. There was never too much work for her. Now she feels empty and worthless. A skiing accident has put an end to everything. Her right hand is now paralysed. She now refers to herself as "a cripple". What is she to do now? Sit around in a cafe and wait for her husband?

Logotherapist Viktor Frankl was convinced that our deepest longing was to find meaning in life. If it evades us, we feel empty, bored, and powerless. A loss of meaning leads to an *existential vacuum* or, in the worst case, depression.

Martha sat across from me in our first session. She began with the following complaint: "I do not want anything from life anymore! Everything has become so meaningless and empty. I just hang around every day! In the evening I stare out the window to see if my husband is coming home!" Frankl believed meaning could be found in every situation of life. He emphasised this point in all of his writings and expressed it passionately in his many speeches. But how does an existential therapist communicate this belief and conviction to a client like Martha?

For some, meaning may have an objective reality. This, however, may not necessarily be valid for every person. One cannot prescribe meaning or create it for someone else. Each of us faces the question of what is meaningful and what is not on our own. Meaning is always a possibility, one which appears and disappears throughout our lives. Frankl emphasised that there are numerous possibilities for meaning in every situation but each of us must be open and willing to move towards these possibilities. In order to experience meaning, a person must give her inner consent to the opportunity present before her. Meaning cannot be established if a person approaches a situation half-heartedly and from a distance. Meaning is also not an object, which can be grasped. Only through the use and openness of all our senses do we come close to discovering meaning. In light of these conditions, it is understandable that grasping meaning may pose a problem for some. It is even more understandable when people are already burdened by crises, loss, and pressing decisions. Alfried Längle has developed a method to help people approach and experience meaning in their lives. One of his first publications, titled "Schritte zum existentiellen Sinn" ("Steps towards Existential Meaning") (Längle, 1988) is more commonly known today as the "Sinnerfassungsmethode" ("Method of Grasping Meaning"). Längle developed this method, a method that incorporates many important elements from Frankl's theory of meaning, based upon his many years of therapeutic experience. The method of finding meaning has four steps.

Step 1: Awareness

The process of finding meaning begins with the intake of information and orientation. The first step is awareness of the given situation. Greater awareness occurs when decisions need to be made in everyday life as well as in difficult situations. Or it occurs when a path can no longer be seen and everything becomes meaningless. A person must become aware of the given situation he faces first, followed by a realisation of the opportunities that lie within that situation. Becoming aware of a given situation allows the therapist to ask the following questions: "What is the situation like? What has happened? What are the overall conditions?" A person must try to grasp the facts of the situation with as little prejudice as possible. Further questions then need to be asked about what is possible: "What is possible now? What can be done?" This first step can be difficult because of distorted views, biographic imprints, traumas, or fixed ideas. It can be hard for a person to let go of these and focus on the actual experience.

Step 2: Assessment

When a person tries to assess the measure of meaning in a certain possibility, she must grasp its value. How can a person grasp the value of a possibility? This is done through the establishment of an emotional relationship. A person may then realise the importance of a situation and spontaneously feel its significance without reflection. Längle describes this important process as follows:

> A person emphatically opens their spirit—senses—to the situation, the object, the possibility for action, or to the other person. They then feel the value within themselves, the value of the object for their life in general and for its aim. The more a person opens up to this object, the more they grasp its value. This objective realization turns into an emotional sense for value. (Längle et al., 2000, p. 16)

The following questions address this step of assessment: "What do you feel during this process? How do you experience it? How does it affect you?"

Step 3: Decision

When we are able to sense various avenues for meaning, their differing value, the emotional unveiling of the actual situation and the best possibility in the present moment, we need to practise another essential mental act: we need to make a decision. We need to say "yes" and take a position towards the right possibility. We need to create the prerequisites that will shift the possibility into action. The act of conscious decision is especially important when the best possible action is difficult to do and when it has far-reaching consequences. The action takes on the form of a contract, as if the person signed a contract by acting on the present possibility for meaning. The questions that arise at this step of decision are, "Do I say, 'yes' to this? Do I want to make this kind of decision?"

Step 4: Execution

As a therapist, I have often experienced the following. When a person makes a decision full-heartedly, the realisation and awareness of what is possible is seldom a problem. The decision for action becomes a logical and inevitable consequence of the previous steps. There are, of course, situations where the transition between decision and execution does not flow easily. This is especially the case in difficult situations like the loss of a job, divorce, or abstaining from alcohol. In cases like these, the fourth step in grasping meaning—execution—becomes a focus on finding ways and means to support the chosen path. This includes: developing a plan of action (the consecutive steps necessary for execution), practising the situation, rewards, and imaginative conceptualisation. In the following passages I want to illustrate the method of grasping meaning by drawing on three cases from therapeutic practice. I have chosen these in order to illustrate, through varying situations, the main emphases on themes and goals. It is possible to address these aspects with the method being discussed.

1. Awareness

Martha S.

During the initial hours of therapy there was only one thing that was important to Martha: the fact that everything she had been able to do before her skiing accident she now considered impossible. She was unable to work and, while she lamented this situation, I noticed that she often mentioned things that were important to her such as her housekeeping. This task was physically difficult for her to do and yet she told me her house always looked spic and span. Also of importance was her embroidery—for which she only needed one hand—and the ritual of the Sunday morning breakfast and her visits to the cafe. She got excited when she talked about these things and the significance of these activities became evident. But she only addressed these things on the side, even pejoratively. She talked about these activities as if they were nice hobbies. Without her job as her main activity they were completely worthless. After a few sessions talking about the loss of her job and the subsequent sorrow she felt, I started asking her questions about the hobbies she had mentioned. I asked the "who", "what", "when", and "where" questions in order to get an accurate picture of my client and to see how much time and space these hobbies occupied in her life. I wanted to find out if these hobbies could in fact become something important to her.

I want to use her visits to the cafe as an illustration of the steps in the method of grasping meaning. Martha began describing her favourite cafe to me but was quick to point out that she "would merely observe how busy everyone else was" in comparison to her. In every session that followed, however, she spoke more and more about what she observed at the cafe. She told me which newspapers she read, what kind of cakes she ordered and what she talked about with a friend whom she met with regularly. Her growing "realisation" or awareness of the situation became increasingly broad and differentiated.

Karola M.

Karola was a very attractive young woman. The way she approached other people made her especially attractive. She had a very cultured and warm way of talking to others, and people were usually quite fond of her. Karola's greatest desire was to have a family. She held on to the idea that a person must have a family by the time they reach the age of thirty. Only then would life make any sense, only then would she reach her calling as a woman. This conviction was evident in all her thoughts. When we discussed the biography of her family, it became evident why she held such convictions and would not let go of them. Her parents had filed for divorce when Karola was only two years old and her mother had never gotten over it. She had always made it clear to her daughter that the meaning of life comprised of marriage and family. Because of this, Karola had retreated into her own world to some extent; she was almost depressed. She had done this because she could not motivate herself to do anything productive. Further, she did not want to be around happy and ecstatic people. When she went for a walk in the park or to a restaurant to eat, the picture was always the same: she saw happy couples everywhere. It was worse when she went to a cafe on a Sunday morning: happy families everywhere. She saw parents that loved each other. They were content and fulfilled when they looked at their children. We remained at this first step of "realisation" and aware- ness for some time. The distortions in her outlook became quite evident to me and this is why I placed so much emphasis on the first step. We talked about her point of view and I asked her for examples of what defined being happy and content. She thought about her answer but then noticed her own distorted realisation. "That is just an illusion," she said. It was surprising to me how quickly Karola could give up her idealised conceptions. We then examined her life, one which was filled with various interests and activities. I tried to describe her life as objec- tively as possible. I wanted to mention both the negative and positive aspects. While she often complained and lamented her life, the more we talked the more she was able to see the positive sides to her life as a single woman. She was then able to think about her work, her activities during her leisure time, and her friends.

Hans F.

Hans F. is retired. For decades now he has been separated from his wife. Up to now he has lived out his humble life quite well. He goes on hikes and likes to read. He likes to go to Vienna's typical "Heurigen" taverns and drink the latest vintage of wine. "But the most important thing is that I have a good relationship with my son."

Hans' son was moving to Australia on account of a job. He had sug- gested his father come with him, to "uproot him", as Hans expressed it. Hans could not make up his mind on this subject. We decided to approach this difficult question together. "If I stay here, I will only see him once, maybe twice a year. That would require a lot of readjust- ment!" Until now the two of them had been together once a week, fish- ing or going to the tavern. They had talked a lot. "We could continue to do this in Australia. But we couldn't go to a tavern, and fishing may also prove difficult. The area where my son is going is very dry." Hans F. was accustomed to the way things were in Vienna and was able to participate in his hobbies. "I know my way around here; my roots are here!—But what good is all this without my son?" These were the facts and Hans had already taken them into account. Despite his realisation of these facts, he could not come to a decision on the matter.

2. Assessment

Martha S.

Martha talked a great deal about her visits to the cafe. Now it was time to discover what kind of emotions accompanied Martha's observations and experiences. I not only asked her about the "what" but also about the "how". I asked her about the atmosphere in the cafe, how she felt there and what she liked specifically? She told me that she had acquired a favourite place to sit. From there she could observe all the comings and goings. She described how she sunk back into the seat and ordered her coffee. Coffee was important to her but in the past she had always had to drink it in haste. Now she had the opportunity to spend more time and to make it a conscious experience. I asked her to tell me exactly what she did when the coffee was finally in front of her:

CLIENT: I put two spoons of sugar into my coffee, stir, and drink it.
THERAPIST: Have you ever consciously taken the cup into your hands and felt it? Have you ever smelt it?
C: No, I haven't.
T: Let us try to imagine doing this. Imagine that you are taking your coffee cup into your hands, what do you feel?
C: It's warm, nice and warm.
T: Put your nose right over the cup. What happens?
C: It's moist. The steam rises into my nose. But it smells good. I really like the smell of coffee.
T: And now?
C: I carefully drink for the first time. I like the taste.
T: What does it taste like exactly??
C: It tastes sweet, warm, and pleasant.
T: And when you swallow?
C: The warmth goes all the way down to my stomach.
T: Is that good?
C: Yes, it is. Now that I see it in my imagination, I feel whole and warm.

Throughout our conversation Martha interrupted her answers by saying that all of this did not have any real value. "What kind of significance does something like this have?" I then changed direction. "What would happen if you did not have these activities and experiences, like going to the cafe and working on embroidery?" At first she resisted the question and did not want to face this alternative. "Not much would be different!" she said. But she became quieter and quieter when I asked this question. Then she finally said, "If I did not have these activities I would get depressed quite easily. I would lose my motivation. I would just sit in front of the television." On one occasion she said, "That would not be a good alternative. My life would be over." After this she did not refer to her situation pejoratively; she approached the new areas in her life more intensely—especially her visits to the cafe. These visits sometimes took all afternoon. Her explanations became more extensive and more emotional. She now described her coffee-drinking as follows: "I can already smell my coffee when the waiter comes and I look forward to drinking it. I always scoop off the whipped cream from the top. I let it melt on my tongue. And then I drink the first sip. I let it run down my throat and inhale deeply. Then I think to myself that 'it's quite comfy here'."

Karola M.

In the first step of "realisation" we talked about Karola's numerous activities, hobbies, and achievements. These were areas in which she invested a lot of time and effort. In light of this I tried to assess the worth of these things with her. Karola played the piano, for example, and from what she told me I knew that she had commenced this hobby with intensity and enthusiasm. She had performed her first recital after four months. I asked her how she experienced her playing. She answered, "It was all very nice, but I soon lost my motivation. Why should I keep on playing? Just for myself?" At a later point I tried to recover the positive feelings she had had while playing for her recital. But her answers remained the same. She also added, "It would only be good if my children could accompany me on the piano!" I realised that the messages from her childhood and her fixed ideas did not allow her to feel the value of a given situation. At this point we parted from the method of grasping meaning and turned to working through the obstacles of Karola's biography.

Hans F.

Let us turn to Hans and the two alternatives he was considering. I encouraged him to picture what life would be like in Australia. "Both of us would live in a house on the outskirts of a small town," he stated. "The house looks very nice from the pictures and would be quite comfortable to live in. We could have breakfast on our patio, maybe go on excursions ...". We talked in depth about the atmosphere of a weekend like this, until even I as a listener could sense how good he felt being together with his son and his daughter-in-law. "The whole world seems right to me when we sit and talk and drink." I noticed that Hans focused mainly on the weekends when he talked about being together with his son and daughter-in-law. I gradually approached him with the question of what his life would be like during the week. The mood of Hans F. changed abruptly. He seemed down and his words became clipped. He pictured himself sitting alone in a rocking chair on the patio. He was overcome by a feeling of being lost. He could hardly imagine any activities. It turned out he could hardly speak English and doubted very much that he would be able to learn. He therefore pictured himself as secluded and sitting around his son's property. He was hesitant—as if he did not want to say it out loud—to confess that he would need an area of his own in which he could move around. The longer we thought about this picture the more imprisoned and disoriented he felt. When he reached this point his thoughts returned to Vienna where he did not picture himself as passive or inactive. He was surprised to realise that his week was actually quite full with activities. He had never really realised this. We looked at the separate activities in greater detail and discovered that Hans was in contact with only a few people. But his friendships with these few had lasted for decades. "Of course my relationship to my son is closer than to these people. But they are old buddies. I can do things with them and they were there for me when I needed their help." "And if you went to Australia?" "I would miss them immensely," Hans F. said quickly. He surprised even himself with his next comment, "I was never really conscious of this fact. I would miss them! With regard to my son it was always clear." He reflected. "It's not just about the friends. It's about what we do together, like going to a tavern and joking around. The entire atmosphere would be different with other people. I can't imagine doing that somewhere else with other people." The longer we talked about this imagined picture the value of Hans F.'s connection to his home became more evident.

3. Decision

Martha S.

For Martha it was now possible to distinguish between essential things, those that made her happy, and things that did not. She was able to do this on account of our efforts to feel and evaluate various activities. She now knew how she would feel if she just slacked off and gave up. Joy had re-entered her life and this could be seen in her visits to the cafe and in other areas as well. She had always resisted calling these things her life. All these things were nice but they could never compete with the value of her profession. One day that changed. She came and told me that she had seen photographs of herself taken during the time she was working. "I was shocked to discover how stressed I looked in those pictures. I then thought to myself that this is a great opportunity for me. I can live a good life now. After all the work and overtime, I can now enjoy life." She had spontaneously decided to accept her new living situation and to think of it as valuable.

Hans F.

The more we pictured a life for Hans F. in Australia, the more his mood seemed to change. The depressive lifelessness abated and a different mood came over him. He was still sad but somewhat livelier now. I told him about my observations. He agreed: "Yes, it's true." He was fighting off tears. "You know the longer I think about it the more clear my thoughts are and the more I know what my decision must be. Actually, I have known it all along. My roots are here, everything I do and think about belongs here. You can't just uproot something like that." The direction of his decision became evident. The sessions that followed dealt with the sorrow of being so distant from his son. This also helped make the decision more concrete.

4. Execution

Martha S.

Martha was now free to execute her plans. There were no more obstacles to remove. During the long process of assessment, she had begun to turn towards new areas and fill them with life. When she finally made her decision, she had sufficient strength and conviction.

Hans F.

The decision had been made. But Hans still needed some support to convincingly carry out his decision. He had to let his son know about it. I supported him in the process of writing a letter. He was quite worried that communication between him and his son would break down. When he realised that he could not only write letters regularly but also spontaneously share experiences and thoughts on the phone, he was greatly relieved. He calculated how often he could travel to Australia. We talked specifically about his spare time on the weekends in order to prevent him from sinking into a depression. He had always been with his son on those days. We also talked about informing his friends about his decision. They would all meet together and he would tell them about his plans. Their support and constant contact would be very important to him now.

Three fates, three paths, three outcomes

For Martha S. and Hans F. it was possible to reach a solution using the method of grasping meaning. When talks started, Martha S. was in a typical situation for the issue of meaning to arise: there was a radical loss of meaning due to the loss of a great value in her life. Different areas of her life emerged that suggested new meaning and contentment. But she needed consultative talks in order to turn those opportunities into real sensual experiences. The method of grasping meaning supplied the tools for this process. She took one step at a time in order to fill the vacancy of meaning with a new and fulfilling daily life. Hans F.'s problem also represented a typical situation. The question of meaning demanded an urgent answer. There was a conflict of values. He had to make two decisions on how best to shape his life. Both possibilities seemed equivalent and both seemed to be associated with something negative, this paralysed Hans F. and the process of making a decision was then prolonged. The method of grasping meaning freed Hans of the paralysing consequences and enabled him to assess the possibilities that eventually led him to a decision. The theme and problem of "meaning" is not the only issue for which the application of the meaning-grasping method is prescribed. The personal abilities of the client call for this method as well.

Before the problems of Martha S. and Hans F. surfaced, they had managed their problems and the demands of life very well. They were able to perceive reality, adjust accordingly and deal with the given situations. Karola's situation was different. It was evident when she described her problem that her conceptions of life were fixed and inflexible. It was impossible for her to feel any value in her life. On account of this we abandoned the method of grasping meaning in order to work through previous experiences. These experiences had led her to an inhibiting fixation.

Karola's case demonstrates the limitations of the method of grasping meaning. The emphasis in the logotherapeutic method is on dealing with concrete problems. These people had relatively well-developed personal abilities. A change in the therapeutic approach is necessary, however, in cases of pathological fixations of attitudes and behavioural patterns. In these cases, the close relationship between the consultative level of the method of grasping meaning and the "personal existential analysis" (also developed by Längle) proves especially advantageous. Because the two methods have a similar structure, the therapist has the possibility of switching between the two. If, for example, a therapist cannot proceed using the method of grasping meaning, they are able to switch to the equivalent step in the personal existential analysis. After using this method they may return to the method of grasping meaning, thereby enabling the client to make great strides towards a meaningful and fulfilling existence.

References

Längle, A. (1988). *Entscheidung zum Sein: Viktor E. Frankls Logotherapie in der Praxis*. München: Piper.

Längle, A., Orgler, Ch., Kundi, M. (2000). *Die Existenzskala*. Göttingen: Hogrefe.

Further reading

Frankl, V. E. (1980). *Das Leiden am sinnlosen Leben: Psychotherapie für heute*. Freiburg: Herder.

Frankl, V. E. (1982). *Ärztliche Seelsorge*. Wien: Deuticke.

Frankl, V. E. (1984). *Der leidende Mensch: Anthropologische Grundlagen der Psychotherapie*. Bern: Huber.

Längle, A. (1985). *Wege zum Sinn: Logotherapie als Orientierungshilfe.* München: Piper.

Längle, A. (1987). *Sinnvoll leben: Angewandte Existenzanalyse.* St. Pölten: Niederösterreichisches Pressehaus.

Längle, A. (1990). Methode der existenzanalytischen Psychotherapie: Kasuistik. *Zeitschrift für Klinische Psychologie, Psychopath., Psychotherapie, 38*: 253–262.

Längle, A. (1990). Personale Existenzanalyse. In: *Wertbegegnung* (pp. 133–160). Wien: Tagungsbericht 4 der GLE.

Längle, A. (1991). Was sucht der Mensch, wenn er Sinn sucht? *Daseinsanalyse, 8*: 174–183.

Längle, A. (1999). Existenzanalyse—Die Zustimmung zum Leben finden. *Fundamenta Psychiatrica, 12*: 139–146.

CHAPTER SIX

Crisis: threat and opportunity

Anton Nindl

In our present day and age, the term crisis has become inflated. There are crises in politics, economics, ecology, medicine, and psychology. But there are also individual crises of meaning, the crisis of maturity in adolescence, mid-life crises, or the breakdown of marriages and consequent crises within families. This chapter will deal with the crisis of the individual. We encounter this kind of crisis in consultation and psychotherapy.

Historic retrospective view

Eric Lindemann (1944) was the first to explore the issue of crisis scientifically. He examined the consequences of the Cocoanut Grove fire which resulted in the death of over 140 people. The survivors, as well as the bereaved families, reacted with shock, guilt, grief, and aggression. These reactions demanded psychotherapeutic help. This was especially true when coping with grief (compare e.g., Fartacek & Nindl, 2001). Ciompi (1996) commented on Gerald Caplan's (1964) review of the Lindemann examination. He explored Lindemann's considerations in further depth and is regarded as the "father of modern crisis theory". Erik Eriksson's (1957) psychodynamic perspective on the critical phases of life also falls within this same time period. In addition, Jacobson (1974) worked on important analyses on the theme of crises. Häfner (1978) did similar work in the United States, Cullberg (1978) in Sweden, and Reiter and Strotzka (1977) in Austria, to name just a few. More recent approaches such as Ciompi (1996) make reference to chaos theory. Intense analyses in post-traumatic stress disorder (PTSD) have lead to concepts of acute treatment. These concepts include elements of emergency and crisis therapy (e.g., Malt & Weisaeth, 1991).

Crisis characteristics

It is not easy to define the term crisis. In reference to Caplan (1964), we could view crisis as an expression and reaction of being over-burdened. In this sense, an event triggers the crisis and it becomes impossible for the person to cope with it using his usual potentialities for problem-solving. In existential analysis we view crisis similarly, namely, as an event that cannot be handled using the usual coping strategies. The person is in a state where he has no possibility of constructively changing something. He remains at a reactive level and loses his personal abilities. Therapeutic assistance should work immediately on the present state and condition of the client in order to prevent irreversible damage. The term crisis refers to a turning point: the entire condition may turn towards the positive or the negative. Crises are polar phenomena. This is expressed in the written characters of the Chinese language. The Chinese word for crisis is *wei-ji*. *Wei* means threat; *ji* means opportunity or chance.

Crises often appear suddenly, almost as a surprise. They are experienced as a threat and often connected to loss or injury. A crisis shakes long-held values and aims, causes fear and helplessness, yet at the same time it demands immediate decisions (Reiter & Strotzka, 1977). Every crisis leads to a somewhat *feeble state*. This state also reveals itself in the social life of a person. Usual behavioural patterns like going to work, housekeeping, eating at a certain time, sleeping, and waking, for example, may be replaced by extremely inadequate behaviour that results in regressive, suicidal, or aggressive conduct. A crisis causes a person to be easily swayed and influenced. Small causes may have great effects. A minor or meaningless conflict may lead to suicide or aggression. On account of this, the threat of chronic disease is immanent. According to Häfner (1978), the main reasons for this are continuous strain and burden, material or social loss, social conditioning (drug and alcohol abuse or confirmation through people of similar mindset). A crisis, as mentioned earlier, is either a *threat* or an *opportunity*. Suicidal behaviour or the outbreak of a psychological disease may be a threat or a danger. Opportunities, on the other hand, may come in the form of getting-to-know-oneself more intimately and the further development of personality.

When and where does a person encounter a crisis? One often encounters states of high excitement due to institutional crises, the influence of alcohol, grief, sorrow, depression, suicide, or suicide attempts. In my therapeutic experience, such states are caused predominantly by unfaithfulness, abandonment, experiences of loss, and changes in life. These insights lead to certain consequences for crisis intervention. But so far no agreement has been reached as to what these consequences should be and how crisis intervention should be separated from short-term psychotherapy or emergency psychiatry. Nonetheless, there are commonalities which can be named as characteristics of crisis intervention (compare Schnyder, 1996):

- Crisis intervention must occur *immediately* and it must be *flexible*.
- A fundamental element is the focus on *current issues*.
- Crisis intervention occurs within a *limited time frame*.
- *Step-by-step* models are regarded as good models.
- There must be an *active and direct therapeutic attitude*, but it should not necessarily be directive.
- Crisis intervention does not belong strictly to the medical field—*interdisciplinary* teams are well suited for this.
- Crisis intervention is not only aimed at the individual, but also incorporates *measures* taken from the client's *social environment*.

I want to address the concrete steps of crisis intervention so as not to evade the complaint of Henseler (1981) who said: "Everyone is talking about crisis intervention, but no one explains how to do it!"

Methodical approach

Entering the relationship

During *first* contact with the client, a therapist should be as open as possible. This is important for therapy in order to establish a calm and clear mindset and to achieve the necessary emotional relief. This enables the therapist to get a clear view of what has happened in the past. At the same time, the therapist must aim at creating the factual preconditions for a constructive dialogue. With regard to institutional settings, one must greet the client by introducing himself, stating his name and title. The therapist should also explain the setting. I might say, for example: "We have an hour of time. Would you like your daughter to be present during our talk? Please, take a seat."

It is typical for clients to lose the overall picture of their situation when they are in a crisis. They are often overwhelmed by contradictory feelings. On account of being reserved and taciturn due to the pain of the crisis, the client needs someone to lead her carefully and offer structures. This does not imply that the client should be repressively commanded, which often occurs. However, the therapist who stands on solid ground needs to exercise a firm hand in order to reach out to the person who is "drowning in the swamp", figuratively speaking. It may be the case that the therapist needs to exercise immediate measures of protection such as medical assistance. At this point the help of the therapist should be like a strong rope in an emergency situation. It is important to give clear advice like: "Remain where you are and wait until your husband has gone to work." A clear methodical approach supplies stability and brings about a calming and relaxing effect. The position and attitude of the therapist is a signal. That signal should say: "Your presence here is completely understandable and natural. It is a necessary consequence of your situation."

I usually commence my sessions with a client by asking how she is doing: "Mrs. Bauer, how are you doing at this moment?" I introduce myself as a whole person by addressing the client at the emotional level. I present myself as someone who is interested in the condition of my client and one who provides emotional relief at the same time. After discussing the effects and emotions, we turn to what has happened. We focus on reality: "Are you able to tell me what happened exactly?" While the client explains the situation, I try to take a position with respect to her reality. I might say: "Yes, that sounds really bad!" The message I am sending the client is: "I am here for you. I am on your side. I can bear what has happened to you. I can also bear you in your need" (compare Tutsch, 1993; Längle, 1997).

Problem analysis

After this first step of emotional relief, we come to the *situational analysis* (Schnyder, 1996). This step is about finding out what is actually going on and what the problem is really about. What are the triggering mechanisms of the crisis? There are often specific burdens in the area of social relationships. There may be relationship conflicts. There may be threats or losses on account of a break-up, divorce, or death. There may also be a diagnosis of a serious disease, an accident, or the experience of a violent act. Perhaps a person has been dismissed from his job, has problems on account of debt, or quarrels over inheritance. Migrants, for example, often face the threat of deportation.

What is the current living situation of my client? In which phase of life is she? How is she connected emotionally to the surrounding environment? How are her social contacts? Does she have relationships with family members, friends, or neighbours? What is her work situation like? Is the client a housewife and thereby materially depended on her husband, for example? What does she do in her spare time? These areas shed light on the *background of the crisis*. They may indicate the sensitivity of the client with regard to the triggering mechanism of the crisis and shed further light on already existent and possible resources.

Which *resources* can be found? What kind of cognitive and practical life skills are present? Is the client physically healthy? Which ethical and religious values make the person feel stable and secure? For example, the experience of having gone through a crisis in the past may have a protective effect by producing a hopeful and assured attitude towards life and the ability to bear certain burdens. In addition, positive human relationships as well as financial security are areas that supply significant resources for the client.

The next step is to summarise the current situation together. My client and I try to find understandable words for the current crisis. The summary may go something like this:

> Last Thursday your husband confessed to you that he has a girl-friend and will leave the family on account of her. You felt as though you had been struck by lightning. You could not bear or handle this situation. You could not understand how he could do something like this to you. You feel helpless and desperate and the only thing on your mind is to get your husband back, despite everything that has happened.

All of this serves the purpose of transporting the client out of a state of "this cannot be real", into a state of "this is the way things are". The client should develop a clearer understanding of the crisis and accept the fact that she is in a crisis.

While we approach the reality of the situation together, we also find each other. At this point, the client and I must stop looking at the mere facts of the problem presented and allow closeness into our relationship (compare Längle, 1997). "What is it that hurts so much?"—This kind of question enables the client to get closer to herself and see the value in what has been lost. The client may now turn to the lost relationship. To do this she needs the empathy of the therapist. This particular phase of therapy tries to help the client express her feelings of sorrow, pain, hurt, shame, fear, guilt, perhaps even anger and bitterness. It is better to express these feelings than to let them brood on the inside. This would cause tension and promote disease. The attitude of the therapist should express the following: "I am someone who is touched and interested in you. I am a person who thinks you are important." One must always consider that a crisis may cause a shift in fundamental values. And this poses the question: "Is it still a good thing for me to exist?" The position of the therapist should be: "Yes, it is good. I see something in you that you cannot see yourself at this time." This position is what Cullberg calls *deputised hope* (Cullberg, 1978, pp. 25–34). At this point in therapy it may be advantageous for the therapist to set forth a goal. For example:

> In the next six weeks it should be possible for Mrs. Bauer to deal with the marriage situation. She should be able to settle the matter so that she may know which direction to go in. A talk with both husband and wife will aid the process. Mrs Bauer should come to the point at which she is at least able to imagine a life without her husband.

For the therapist it is very important to keep the threats and dangers of crises in mind while the client is in the *reaction phase* (compare Tutsch, 1993). Where is my client endangered? Where does she "drift off"? Where does she move too fast? Does she have suicidal tendencies? Could a psychological disease break out? Is there a danger of a chronic illness due to the burdens that have remained upon the person for a long period of time? Will this cause material and social loss? The therapist needs to differentiate and to understand (sometimes even to explain) in order to show his client the possible threats and dangers that may arise—alcohol abuse, for example.

Work phase

The focus of the *work phase* is on personal resources. It is about finding and strengthening what the person calls her own (compare Längle, 1997). What could actually help the client to overcome the situation? What is the client's precise problem? How does she contribute to the ongoing existence of the problem? What can she do about it? What would be a realistic position for her to take towards the situation but also towards herself and her life? Does the client want to remain a victim? If this is not the case, what are the consequences? What should be done in the current situation? What is hindering the client from putting these things into practice?

Distancing techniques may be helpful: "What would you suggest to a good friend?" or "If you were the good friend, what would you tell yourself?" Techniques such as these allow the client to achieve a certain degree of self-distance. The therapeutic position is marked by assurance and esteem for the client. The message is: "You are allowed to be the way you are. You may assure yourself of this. I want to help you so you can be yourself again." Generally, familiar potentialities are reactivated at this point. The consulter or therapist strengthens, encourages, takes a position, takes a step back and tries to promote the client's own initiative.

A new orientation for life

The next step is about letting the client take the initiative. It is about letting her take the necessary steps. The client should let go of the passive attitude of expectation, making her dependent upon a husband, for example. Instead, the client is encouraged to take her life into her own hands. This step is, in a sense, a new direction for life. It is supposed to enable the client to actively shape her existence. In the example presented, the meaning and significance of the crisis had become conscious to the client. She knew she had to change her life at a functional level. In the meantime, the client also agreed that a part-time job would be a good idea. She thought to herself: "I will not be there for everybody at every moment of the day." The client was now self-assured and believed she was able to deal with her situation. She looked forward to a short vacation, one she had spontaneously arranged for herself. We agreed that she would contact me after approximately one month.

When she phoned, she was confident and hopeful. We agreed to have a concluding talk after another month.

A concluding session two or three months after the crisis intervention has proven to be a reliable method. Various authors have referred to this (e.g., Sonneck, 1995; Schnyder, 1996). The follow-up contact should discuss the experiences and behaviour of the client since the last session. How is she handling her life? What has changed? How does she view her crisis in retrospect? How does she evaluate her way of coping with the crisis in retrospect? Is there an indication for long-term psychotherapy? What are the situational conditions like? The client in my example was able to forego long-term, consultative-therapeutic support. This became evident in our concluding session. In fact, her husband came back and decided to stay with her and the family. She does not conceal the fact that tensions arise from time to time. But she is able to handle these tensions well. She is self-assured and hopeful, and believes that in the long run her marriage and family life will improve even more.

From my experience, the process of handling a crisis does not always end as well as this example. The progression of steps may vary depending upon the urgency of an issue. No one is exempt from finding their personal answer to a crisis. Even when life takes away a person's ability to speak, sooner or later he must respond. In his own unique way, Erich Fried encourages us to respond:

Undoing

Being able to exhale
your bad luck

to deeply exhale
in order to
inhale again

And perhaps to even speak about one's bad luck
to speak about it using words
real words
connected words with meaning
words which someone else

may perhaps understand
or could understand

And being able to cry

That would almost be
a stroke of
good luck

References

Caplan, G. (1964). *Principles of Preventive Psychiatry*. New York: Basic.

Ciompi, L. (1996). Krisentheorie heute: Eine Übersicht. In: U. Schnyder and J. D. Sauvant (Eds.), *Krisenintervention in der Psychiatrie 2* (pp. 13–25). Bern: Huber.

Cullberg, J. (1978). Krisen und Krisentherapie. *Psychiatr. Prax.*, 5: 25–34.

Eriksson, E. (1957). *Kindheit und Gesellschaft*. Zürich: Pan Verlag.

Fartacek, R., & Nindl, A. (2001). Normale und abnorme Trauerreaktionen. In: H. Katschnig & U. Demal (Eds.), *Trauer und Depression: Wo hört das eine auf, wo fängt das andere an?* (pp. 25–41). Wien: Facultas.

Fried, E. (1997). Aufhebung. In: *Beunruhigungen*. Berlin: Wagenbach.

Häfner, H. (1978). Krisenintervention und Notfallversorgung in der Psychiatrie. In: H. J. Haase (Ed.), *Krisenintervention in der Psychiatrie*. Stuttgart/ New York: Schattauer.

Henseler, H. (1981). Krisenintervention—Vom bewussten zum unbewussten Konflikt des Suizidanten. In: H. Henseler and C. Reimer (Eds.), *Selbstmordgefährdung: Zur Psychodynamik und Psychotherapie*. Stuttgart: frommann-holzboog.

Jacobson, G. F. (1974). Programs and techniques of crisis intervention. In: S. Arieti (Ed.), *American Handbook of Psychiatry* (Vol. 2, Chapter 55). New York: Basic.

Längle, A. (1997). *Existenzanalytische Krisenintervention*. Unveröff. Arbeitsblatt.

Lindemann, E. (1944). Symptomatology and management of acute grief. *American Journal of Psychiatry*, 101: 141–148.

Malt, U. F., & Weisaeth, L. (1991). Disaster psychiatry and traumatic stress studies in Norway: History, current status and future. *Acta Psychiatrica Scandinavica*, 80: Suppl. 355, 7–12.

Reiter, L., & Strotzka, H. (1977). Der Begriff der Krise: Ideengeschichtliche Wurzeln und aktuelle Probleme des Krisenbegriffes. *Psychiatria Clinica*, 10: 7–26.

Schnyder, U. (1996). Ambulante Krisenintervention. In: U. Schnyder and J. D. Sauvant (Eds.), *Krisenintervention in der Psychiatrie 2* (pp. 55–74). Bern: Huber.

Sonneck, G. (1995). *Krisenintervention und Suizidverhütung: Ein Leitfaden für den Umgang mit Menschen in Krisen.* Wien: Facultas.

Tutsch, L. (1993). *Krisenintervention.* Herbstakademie der GLE. Seminarmitschrift.

CHAPTER SEVEN

Fear: the royal road to existence—what hides behind fundamental fear and anticipatory anxiety?

Silvia Längle

When one considers the issue of fear, an obvious approach is to examine the causes of fear and simply rid ourselves of them. We would not have to deal with fear any longer. There would be no need for us to be afraid anymore. Fear would have been thoroughly uprooted and disposed of. What then is in fear, if anything at all, that is worthy of consideration and thought?

What is fear?

Fear is unpleasant, even absurd at times. It tortures us, blocks us, causes us to flee, to sweat, to go weak at the knees, causes our stomachs to growl, makes breathing difficult, and causes our hearts to pound ...

Fear as a signal

First of all, fear is an indication of danger or physical threat. This indication is not trivial; it cannot be pushed aside. But as a spontaneous inner motion, fear forces a person to react and to act. It is relentless and cannot be ignored. In this sense, fear secures the physical survival of the person. In fact, ancestral history and brain physiology regard this indicating fear as the root of experiential fear (cf. Morschitzky, 2002).

Indicating fear appears when a person encounters a dangerous enemy or situation. As humans, we are somatically and psychologically well equipped, and can therefore overcome situations we encounter. The body spontaneously increases its metabolism and makes an immediate reaction possible. This reaction occurs long before any conscious thinking takes place. It is the basis for many coping reactions and a dependable form of protection. This alarm leads to the well-known reactions of flight, avoidance, even destructive aggression or a reflex to play dead. An unconscious evaluation of the danger and one's own psychophysical condition determines which one of these coping reactions (cf. A. Längle, 1998) is appropriate. Correctional (if necessary) and responsible action occurs after the initial reaction. This secondary type of behaviour goes beyond coping mechanisms and lets the person deal more freely with the situation.

An existential trace

Fear not only causes us to actively worry about our survival, it also instils the inextinguishable experience of vulnerability and death. It lets us feel that death and danger are a part of life. Every fear a person has lived through leaves an existentially significant trace behind. Fear demands an answer from us:

> How do we deal with the fact that we are so vulnerable and mortal?
> What position do we take towards this fact?

Every fear confronts us with a twofold task. First, overcoming the situation, and second, carrying the significance of it inside of ourselves and dealing with it.

Fear makes us weak—shaking knees, a pounding heart, difficulty breathing, and a focused expression in one's eyes, all testify to this. I experience myself as tiny, face to face with a monstrous animal, powerless and without protection, confronted with war and terror. I feel shame when my face turns red, when I have to offer my sweaty hand to my boss. I feel helpless and ashamed when I have to talk in front of a large crowd. When I am denied or when others do not accept me, I feel worthless.

All of these fearful experiences are unpleasant, even threatening. They cause insecurity. A person therefore tries to avoid them. This brings us to a fundamental form of pathological fear, namely, the fear of expectation (cf. V. Frankl, 1987, p. 293). This fear of expectation is a fixed form of avoiding fear (cf. also A. Längle, 1996).

Fear of expectation

The character of this kind of fear is its lurking expectation of threat and the efforts taken by the person to avoid it.

If a person experiences something shameful, something which makes him feel helpless, he experiences it as an attack on his person. He views the world as an inscrutable place. He is scared and insecure. He loses faith in overcoming such a threat and subsequently loses his inner grip and security. As a further consequence, his will to live is damaged. He can no longer take on the fearful event that shook him. Ultimately, the person merely tries to avoid it. A confrontation with this type of fear makes a person feel overrun, even annihilated.

If a person does not regain his grip and his courage does not emerge, he will continue to have a fearful attitude. Such a person never wants to experience such a feeling of perdition and weakness again. He therefore lives in fearful expectation; he has the fear of expectation. This fear is accompanied by a feeling which says: "I just can't take it any longer."

The fear of flying is a good example of this type of fear. Such fear is in fact quite common. The fear of flying is most often a fear of expectation. The event that leads to the first outbreak of fear may be of differing nature. It may be the prior experience of a turbulent flight or the experience of being cramped in, not being able to move around enough. Or it may evoke the experience of being in a situation that one cannot get out of—such as when the doors finally close. It may also be merely the *thought* of being boxed in, the thought of not being able to get out anymore. It may be the thought of flying, of not having any solid ground beneath one's feet anymore. The thought of a plane crash may be similarly dramatic: the vision of experiencing the minutes prior to certain death. Thoughts like these can be a terrible torment. Merely the thought of flying causes some people to be afraid and tense.

A mechanism is set in motion in order to deal with such rising fear. A person develops an inner attitude of protection. This attitude causes a person to avoid the fearful experience and simply not place herself in such a fearful situation or event any longer. The fear of expectancy is locally narrowed and her "free-floating fear" is focused or fixed on a certain object or event. This creates security. The threat is boxed in and the fear may be avoided. The person then avoids her fear by never setting foot inside an aeroplane again.

Other forms of the fear of expectation are the fear of enclosed spaces (claustrophobia), the fear of subways, the fear of trains, and the fear of elevators. Or it may be the fear of wide open spaces (agoraphobia), of masses of people (a concert hall or a fair, for example). The fear of expectation may take on the form of a social phobia. Such a person has a general fear of meeting other people. Quite often people are also afraid of heights, of darkness, and of certain animals, like snakes, spiders, and dogs.

Whenever a certain fear is localised and refers to a specific situation or object, the psychologist speaks of a phobia. In a sense, it is possible to develop a phobia about anything: a person may have a phobia about Aids, BSE, a malignant growth, bacteria, dust, pointy objects, doing the washing, noise, books, and even being in love. When you look up "phobia" on the Internet, there are over 500 professional categories of specific phobias.

Usually the person who has this type of fear even finds her own strong, fearful reactions quite ridiculous. Nonetheless, she is helpless and powerless on account of them. A phobia means massive, intense feelings of suffering coupled with restricted action.

When we compare the statistics about phobias with real causes of accidents and death, however, there are in fact great differences. A January 2003 article by Reto U. Schneider in the *Neue Zürcher Zeitung* (NZZ) ("New Zurich Newspaper") published a list of phobias from various sources titled "Achtung, Kokosnuss!" ("Beware of the Coconut!"). Here are a few excerpts from the article:

> According to a survey on fear (U.S.A. 1999) 63% of adults stated that they were afraid of snakes; 55% were afraid of heights; 41% were afraid of being alone in a forest; 37% were afraid of spiders; 35% of flies; 21% were afraid of dogs.
>
> Yet the average number of yearly deaths on account of spider or snake bites in the U.S. is only 10. Dog bites lead to 15 deaths

a year; wasp or bee stings kill 44 people; lightning strikes down 141 people.

Other surprising facts:

> The amount of deaths (worldwide) on account of shark attacks is: 10.
> The amount of deaths due to falling coconuts (worldwide) is: 150.

What does this say about our knowledge of fear?

Are we really afraid of the things that we appear to be afraid of? Fears are difficult to understand. What is at the root of them? Is the cause really what it appears to be? I want to return to this issue a bit later.

Fundamental fear

After examining the fear of expectation, we now come to fundamental fear. Fear of expectation is a secondary phenomenon. The primary phenomenon is fundamental fear.

> A disturbance of foundational essentials causes fundamental fear. These essentials give us room to live and provide security. They allow us to simply be.
> A disturbance of this type shakes up life and opens up an abyss. Our sense of security is disturbed. It is the threat or the actuality of no longer being secure in that which "is" (ontology). (Cf. Längle, 2016)

But how is this fear experienced exactly? It begins with a feeling of losing the ground beneath one's feet, of being exposed to and at the mercy of something. A person loses the trusted structures that gave him orientation in life.

A physical threat from the outside, such as violence, war and terror, or the outbreak of a serious disease, may cause this fear. Its cause is a weakening experience of infirmity. It may also occur when our trust in another has been shaken, when we distrust both our relationship and our partner. Or when certain goals in life begin to unravel: the loss of a job, material security, familiar environment, our home, or our abilities as we grow older, including the ability to think clearly. This kind of fear may occur when we are overwhelmed by ungraspable, unexplainable feelings or inner experiences. In cases like these, we experience a disturbance of security. We can also develop a permanent, foundational attitude of fear when we lack the feeling of being cared for. This attitude develops when we do not experience a sufficient sense of security as a child.

During the course of one's life there is a continuous open sphere of trust and distrust. This sphere is influenced by experiences, either promoting trust or distrust. Fundamental fear develops within this sphere. It is the borders of this sphere that make up the fundamental conditions of life. This sphere extends to the world, to our relationships, as well as to the world inside of us.

We can depend on the rhythm of the seasons. After every winter there will be a time of spring when everything blooms again. Nonetheless, a frost may destroy the blossoms, a drought may threaten the harvest, and a flood may destroy everything. We depend on economic stability and trust that our stocks will rise on the financial market. But, if this fails, we may end up losing a lot. We depend upon each other and suffer when we discover the limitations of trust.

Something always remains open in life; there is no ultimate security. We live and trust in our liveliness, but at the same time we know about our mortality. In this sense, fundamental fear is part of the existential-analytic understanding of humankind. We are necessarily placed in a sphere of indissoluble tension. We sway between being and non-being, between life and "nothing at all":

> When a person experiences extreme stress, fundamental fear may be awakened. It may hinder life, paralyze us, scare us and cause thoughts, actions and feelings of panic. This may occur on a broad level and in various areas of life. Or it may take the form of a "hole in the world". Fundamental fear (as a phobia) may break through this hole into our existence. (Cf. Längle, 2013)

The finality and unpredictability of our existence always confronts us with a question: "What are we to do about it?" Fundamental fear refers to this existential question: "How do we deal creatively with the things that are given to us?"

Fear demands an answer. It demands the taking of a position; it demands a *being* which is there and opposes it. It directs our gaze towards those parts that are empty in our life, where we have received nothing in life, where fundamental conditions of existence have not been met and where we lack a fundamental experience of security.

The concrete message of fear

As humans, we must confront fearful experiences and the fact that there is no absolute security. We must realise that life is uncontrollable. We are constantly confronted with new people and things and in our own personal way we must respond with trust. This trust is found in the experience of a final security.

A trusting attitude allows a person to overcome the remainder of her insecurity. Normally a person never loses her trust. Courage and an evaluation of the risks make up the vital basis of this trust. Trust builds a bridge over the chasm of insecurity, the chasm between the trusting in one's own powers and the taking of calculated risk.

On the other hand, the pathological form of this brings about a certain feeling which says that "everything and anything can happen at any time". This leads to a distortion of reality. In a scenario such as this, even possibilities are seen as part of reality. A person does not experience things as possibility but rather as certainty.

The fear of flying as an example

Using the example of the fear of flying, I want to point out the different forms and appearances of fear. The act of flying is especially well suited for a projection of existing latent fear.

The outbreak of *fundamental* fear expressed itself in the following case:

> Mr. K. wanted to go on vacation. He usually did this every year. When he bought a ticket to Thailand, he was very excited about his travel plans. But a problem arose when, two weeks prior to his take-off, Lauda Air had a disastrous plane crash over and are of Thai jungle. All passengers on board the jumbo jet lost their lives. This event affected Mr. K. deeply and, as a consequence, he was no longer joyful about his anticipated trip. He wanted to cancel it. But there were other feelings inside of him; he was not just deeply

moved. This accident was like a slap in the face for him. He could not fathom the fact that this could happen. Prior to this accident he never gave much thought to security issues. After all, flying was one of the safest ways to travel. "But now—whom can I still trust? An accident may happen anytime!" He almost believed that a flight across the jungle necessarily ended in catastrophe. "Lord only knows what the safety precautions are on such a long flight. Something, anything may happen at any given time!" And finally: "Is there any mode of transportation that a person can still safely use?" Even in his car he did not feel secure anymore. He loved his car and had always felt it to be his second home. But now he felt like he was at the mercy of the world, he felt unprotected. It was hard for him to fall asleep. He was discouraged and unmotivated when he had to take on new tasks. Now he had to decide what to do with his vacation. He felt powerless, stuck and paralysed. He had never experienced something like this before.

When fundamental fear breaks out, it causes fragility and insecurity. *Fear of expectation*, on the other hand, is marked by a blocking attitude towards fear. A person fights and wrestles with the expectation of fear. He often senses an outbreak of threat and insecurity but, at the same time, he tries to avoid and escape it. Fundamental fear has the tendency to spread into all areas of a person's life. It is the basic experience of being shaken at the foundation of one's existence. The fear of expectation limits the fear and binds it thematically to a certain area of life. On account of this limitation, there may be areas of one's life that are not affected by fear. The limitation offers a pragmatic solution to avoiding the fear. Yet limiting the fear to an object or event is also part of the nature of the fear of expectation.

A fear of flying may also develop on account of the dynamics of a fear of expectation. The cause of this fear will be thematically rooted in biographical issues.

Themes of fear in light of the three personal fundamental motivations

A. Längle's existential-analytic model of the fundamental motivations supplies an understanding of these "issues" and topics, of the fear of expectation and of fundamental fear.

The *first fundamental motivation* deals with fundamental fear. This first motivation is the conflict of existence, the conflict between everything that exists and with the fact that it exists. This is the actual nature of fear as fear is essentially about existence and the threat to that existence. In this sense, the conflict provides the basis for understanding fundamental fear; the experiences that oppose and work against fear; and the basic experiences of security, like meeting someone who is sufficiently trustworthy, or finding security in one's own existence and within the body.

The *second fundamental motivation* deals with closeness and the beginning of relationships. It deals with the experience of what is valuable and the experience of a fundamental value. In this stage, a person is afraid to lose something which is dear to him and close to his heart. A person has the sensation of free-falling when his closest relationships fall apart. Changes in the area of relationships always mean a loss of security but, at the same time, new opportunities open up. If a person experiences a threat to relationships and he simply cannot or will not give these relationships up, then the loss of a relationship means a loss of a pivotal and essential support.

Fear has its potential in the threat of loss. But essentially the potential lies in the value that a person gives to a relationship, especially if this is an exaggerated value. The fear is also increased if the person feels and senses that he could never bear the loss of such a value. When values are extremely emphasised, they cause a standstill and a crippling of liveliness. The cycle of the fear of expectation is commenced by this attitude: "If only that one scary thing, which threatens the most important and most valuable aspect of my life, would not happen." A feeling of catastrophe is often connected with this: "Anything can happen but not that. That would be the worst!" The following example illustrates this.

A woman described her fear of flying when she was a young girl. This woman flew quite regularly with her family. As a child she had always liked these vacations. At one point she overheard someone saying that planes could crash. This made her uneasy. Her uneasiness developed into a strong fear of flying. From this moment on, she huddled in her seat and flights became torturous for her.

A case such as this requires a confrontational method of therapy. The girl's fear of flying was a very understandable and obvious fear. At the same time, it was very strong. The therapist needed to understand what moved the girl emotionally in these situations. He needed to know what it was like for her in this situation, what it felt like. She was tortured by repeated visions of the plane crashing, seeing how it fell from the sky and smashed to pieces on the ground. To her childlike mind, it seemed helpful to pull her legs up to her chest in order to protect herself from the crash. She thought she would survive the crash if she did this. Another torturous thought was surviving the crash while her parents died. To be left alone, to lose that closeness and security, really scared her. For many years she did not let go of this idea. Her fear of flying became an outlet for her fear of abandonment and her fear of loneliness. She only became conscious of this when she found out what her fear of flying expressed.

Let us now turn to the *third fundamental motivation*. This is the stage of being a unique self. It is the struggle between self and others. The self needs to be separated from others in order to develop. It needs protection. This particular area of life is especially sensitive to limitations, requirements, and pressure. The self is threatened when no one notices or respects it and when there is not enough room for reciprocal feelings. The self is also threatened when it is at the mercy of the world, when it has too much space, when it is set on a high plane into a great vastness and disconnected from the outside world. Too much freedom and not enough nourishment make the self "dizzy".

The concrete possibilities, the space for becoming a self and the foundation of personhood are all lost within these extremes. A person feels like he is up against a wall or lost in a mist. Experiences like these lead to claustrophobia, agoraphobia, acrophobia, to a fear of heights, and to social phobia.

Consider the following illustration: A woman of about fifty-nine wanted to travel to a foreign country to visit her daughter. Her only problem was flying in a plane. Why had she avoided flying for so long? For her it was the feeling of being overcrowded, of being locked into a crowded room. Even the generous space of first class did not improve her mood a great deal. She still felt unprotected. It troubled her that she could not leave the plane whenever she wanted to or felt the urge to. It was the same in similar situations on the ground. Breathing became difficult. She was restless and afraid of collapsing. This she wanted to avoid at all cost. It would be unbearable for her to be so miserable in public. If this happened, she would feel enormously unprotected and could not handle the situation. How terrible it would be if everyone stared at her. It would even be terrible if someone lovingly looked out for her. It would not comfort or relieve her. Her home was the only place that provided her with comfort in such a state of suffering and weakness. Here she felt secure and protected. Any public appearances, by contrast, would feel shameful.

The value of fear

From an existential-analytic point of view, the value of fear can be described as follows.

The purpose of fear is the "activation" of the person. Fear sets off an alarm. It activates protection and mobilises energy. Fear always warns a person when security is threatened and the "contact to existence" vanishes. Being embedded in existence is the foundation for dynamic liveliness. Fear expresses the loss of the foundation of existence. It reveals a false sense of security and tells us that material possessions do not provide existential security. It warns us when we trust naively.

Fear can therefore be understood as a royal road to existence.

- In the state of fear, when the heart pounds and tension rises, the *body* finds *security* in itself.
- Fear makes us dependent on ourselves and makes us lonely. Fear speaks to the individual person; it refers directly to a person's life. In this sense, fear helps a person to seriously take hold of his own life. This experience is important for the process of *individuation*.
- Fear illuminates our limitations. It teaches us to *let* the things of this world *be*. Fear demands an attitude of ease in order to accept our limitations.
- Fear shows us the fragility of what is apparent. It leaves a trace behind so that we may search for a *final security* and the foundation of all existent things. (cf. also Längle, 1996, p. 12).

References

Frankl, V. (1987). *Ärztliche Seelsorge*. Frankfurt am Main: Fischer.

Längle, A. (1996). Der Mensch auf der Suche nach Halt: Existenzanalyse der Angst. *Existenzanalyse*, *13*: 4–12.

Längle, A. (1998). Verständnis und Therapie der Psychodynamik in der Existenzanalyse. *Existenzanalyse*, *15*: 16–27.

Längle, A. (2016, forthcoming). *Existenzanalyse: Existentielle Zugänge der Psychotherapie*. Wien: Facultas.

Morschitzky, H. (2002). *Angststörungen*. Wien: Springer, 2°.

Schneider Reto, U. (2003). Achtung, Kokosnuss! Wovor wir uns (nicht) fürchten sollten. *Neue Zürcher Zeitung NZZ*, (January): Folio, 17.

CHAPTER EIGHT

"I am afraid of falling out of this world": a case study of a patient with severe mutism and complete social withdrawal

Christian Probst

Previous history

Werner was diagnosed with a "schizophrenic mental deficiency". His mother asked me if I would take over his psychotherapeutic treatment. I had known Werner's family privately for many years. Werner was twenty-six years old at the time.

For five years he had not spoken a word. He would lie in bed all day and only leave it during the night. He got up at midnight and stayed awake until two in the morning but only when the other family members were asleep. He would eat a meal, which his mother had prepared for him, in the kitchen and then listen to heavy metal music for an hour. He was an expert when it came to this type of music. His father would regularly buy him the newest CDs and music magazines. By 2.15 a.m. at the latest Werner was back in bed. From then until midnight the next day, he remained in bed. He bit down hard and kept his mouth shut. He would not eat or drink anything until midnight. The same routine unfolded each day.

At the time Werner weighed 125–150 kg and was 175 cm tall. He could no longer wash himself. Psychiatric nurses came and cleaned him twice a week. He required complete nursing care and received the highest possible amount of government support.

The psychiatrist and psychotherapist who supported Werner visited him only very rarely, about three to four times a year. The therapist did not keep his appointments, postponed them, or else simply stayed away without any notice. Werner was very disappointed on account of this—he felt abandoned.

When his mother asked me if I would take Werner as a patient, I noticed she had high expectations. "Someone has got to take care of him, so he can get well again," she said. Before contacting me she had spoken to her son. Werner knew that I had become a psychotherapist and psychiatrist. He was fine with me visiting because he already knew me from my previous visits to the family. Given my familiarity with the family, I had to ask myself how best to proceed. Did it make sense to take Werner into psychotherapy? How would that work since he had stopped talking five years ago?

On one hand, all the efforts by other therapists and doctors over the last ten years had not led to any improvement. On the other hand, Werner's condition could not get any worse. We had, in fact, nothing to lose. Eventually I agreed to a visit with Werner.

The therapeutic process

I encountered an unpleasant smell as soon as I set foot inside Werner's room. The air was stuffy. Werner sat up in bed and greeted me by raising his hand. He evaded looking at me directly and turned his face to the side. I could only see him from the side and from the back. Werner looked unkempt, his hair unwashed. He had bad breath and body odour. His body seemed spongy and soft.

I sat down at the table beside Werner's bed. We began to communicate. He had a stack of papers and writing utensils lying in front of him. Communication proved difficult. Werner wrote in capital letters and I talked to him. Because of this, therapy sessions took as long as two and a half to three hours. After the third session I changed the form of communication. I had noticed that I was barely able to empathise with Werner's world, his thoughts, and his experience of time. The words I spoke seemed extremely fast compared to Werner's answers. Due to this form of communication I was not able to penetrate into Werner's world. I therefore stopped speaking as well. From then on I sat beside him;

we greeted each other with hand signs and communicated by writing. I now began to sense the strangeness of Werner's world, a world in which he had spent the last five years. The surrounding noises became clearly audible because they were not disturbed by the sound of voices anymore.

At first it seemed to take forever to formulate a sentence and write it down in capital letters. Werner then had to read the sentence, formulate his answer, and write it down. When I left his house after a three-hour session, I felt alienated from the world. I needed a couple of minutes to adjust my senses to the noise of the outside environment.

I now understood, at least partly, what Werner meant when he said that he could not think like other people. He wrote:

> It is as if my brain is wrapped in cotton wool. I feel as if I am con-
> stantly dizzy. I am afraid of falling out of this world. I am afraid of
> not being able to communicate by writing anymore. For years now
> I have been repeating four beats from a heavy metal song in my
> head. The group sings the words "we are". I fear that I might forget
> those words. That would bring everything to an end. Then I could
> not communicate anymore. It is like a compulsion, a curse.

During our initial therapy sessions I tried to find out what Werner had experienced during the last few years. What had contributed to his present condition? Werner refused to waste any time explaining it to me. He was certain that this line of enquiry would not help him. He told me his former doctor knew everything about that sort of thing and I should talk to him.

Working at the foundation of existence

For Werner, it was much more important to deal with daily life as he now experienced it. He could hear his father, mother, and thirteen-year-old sister through the closed door of his room. His parents were hateful and aggressive towards each other. He was afraid that his sister would not be able to bear the pressure and that the same thing might happen to her.

When I felt his fear I placed my hand on his shoulder. At first I felt how tense Werner became when I touched him. After a few moments, however, he became more relaxed. I had the feeling that this gesture was good for him. I spent a great deal of time trying to calm Werner's fears concerning his sister. Her response to their parents was completely different. She was aggressive. In her anger and rage she screamed and fought back. Werner had seldom raised his voice; he tended more towards retreat. He had just stopped speaking when others accused him.

In addition to communicating with Werner, I also tried to get him active to some degree. At first I tried to literally give Werner more room to live. Werner was enormously hindered in the first area of fundamental motivations. It was hard for him to simply be—to exist. Only with great hesitation could he say yes to the first fundamental question of existence: *"I am—can I exist?"* His current foundation of existence began to crumble at this point.

From time to time I suggested that Werner leave his bed during the daytime while I was present. I asked him if he could imagine doing this, if he could get used to such an idea. Werner expressed his fears to me. He was afraid of losing the ground beneath his feet, of feeling dizzy, of falling, collapsing, and even dying as a consequence.

I asked him if he trusted me enough to catch him if that happened. He looked me over and after slight hesitation, he agreed. He sensed that I could support him if he lost his balance. In the security of his room and in my presence, Werner finally decided to get up and walk a few paces. We agreed that Werner would attempt to walk to the window, stay there a while, perhaps take a look at the autumn countryside and, when he had had enough, go back to bed. To his astonishment Werner mastered this task quite well.

During the following sessions it became increasingly easier for Werner to walk around his room in my presence. Pretty soon he was able to leave his room and walk out onto the patio. After two months of therapy, Werner moved freely around the yard. Werner was relieved after our walks in the garden to be back in his room. It was exhausting for him to process all the new impressions. Yet while he had grown accustomed to his room and all that was in it, the monotony had begun to bore him.

When therapy had begun, Werner had been hesitant to make appointments with me, but now it was important to him. We had two appointments per week. He became hopeful about improving his condition. I was especially conscientious when it came to keeping the appointments I had with Werner. Because of this, Werner felt that I truly perceived his situation and was able to bear it. My regular and punctual visits were the basis for Werner's trust in me. His foundation of existence became more stable and supportive.

Access to the quality of existence

Therapy with Werner focused mainly on rediscovering his emotionality. After Werner felt increasingly secure in being able to simply exist, it was now time to focus on the second fundamental motivation of existence: *"I am alive—do I like to live?"* This question became more and more significant in therapy.

In all the years prior to therapy, Werner had learned that it was better for him to repress his emotions. When I asked him what he felt when he listened to music or ate something during the night, for example, he could only reply that it was impossible for him to feel anything at all. He felt empty and burned out on the inside. The only feeling he had felt lately was a paralysing and threatening fear. Yet this fear had begun to recede more and more.

From that point on I started touching the plants and leaves when we walked in the garden and Werner did likewise. Werner learned to feel things again. He felt his environment. He felt the trees, bushes, later on his dog and cat. He caressed them and as a consequence was touched by the response from his environment. He could feel the hardness of tree bark and the softness of his dog's fur again. Werner now liked to stay outside longer. It became clear to him that much time was needed in order to focus on the world again. He needed time to open himself up towards experiences and towards the response of his environment.

With much patience it became possible for Werner to begin a relationship with the world again. His fearful-depressive retreat had given way to an increased joy of life. He often played with his dog now. He played fetch with the dog and even ran around the yard himself. Werner learned to open himself up to valuable experiences again. He managed to formulate his emotions and what touched him on the inside more and more.

Werner's foundation of life and existence were strengthened through the work done in the first and second fundamental motivations. The result was a trusting attitude. Due to the work done in the second fundamental motivation, for example, Werner became increasingly touched and experientially moved by his environment. He then sensed his own existence as something valuable. This resulted in the strengthening of Werner's fundamental value. He was strengthened to such a degree that he did not need to keep his environment at a distance anymore. He could let his surroundings move him and deal with the subsequent rise in emotions.

Much had changed in Werner's life. He got up in the morning. He wanted to get out of bed because there were things awaiting him. His dog wanted to play with him. He wanted to go out into the garden as it had begun to bloom and the spring sun was shining. Werner did not want to miss this and he was happy to be out in the world again.

Meeting other people

The ground Werner had gained, though, soon became too small for him. He was now prepared to leave the protection of the yard and step out onto the street in front of the house. After the first few steps in public Werner sensed a threatening fear.

But this fear was no longer diffuse and unspecific. Werner feared that other people would not accept him. He was afraid of being excluded from society because of his condition. He was not able to speak and could therefore barely communicate with other people. He was afraid of not being accepted by other people on account of his peculiarities, of being laughed at and of not being taken seriously. Werner was convinced that he would never be able to speak again. He was therefore afraid of not being a complete and real person and he despised himself for it.

Werner did not have much confidence in anything he did. The contact he made with the world illuminated how great his deficits were in comparison to normal and healthy people.

Werner had found security and trust in his foundation of existence. He had been strengthened in his fundamental value by experiencing value and self-worth. But now Werner began to doubt himself and his self-worth. The question of the third fundamental motivation of existence became increasingly urgent for him. When he encountered the outer world, he felt a question inside of him: *"I am myself—am I allowed to be this way? Am I allowed to be the unique person I am."* Werner sensed how much he doubted his self-worth. He was afraid of not being taken seriously. He was ashamed when he met other people and afraid of being despised by them.

It was important to confront Werner with concrete situations. In therapy he was to imagine walking into a music store and buying magazines and records. We talked about this situation step by step. Werner thought about how he could protect himself from unpleasant questions and behaviour, how he could distance himself from others and hold his own. Several of these "theoretical exercises" helped Werner to remain with himself, to distance himself from possible hurts and shameless acts within the environment. He was now ready to put theory into practice. During the following therapy session, Werner told me that he had gone to Mediamarkt (a German media store) with his father and everything had worked out wonderfully.

At this point Werner reminded me of an offer I had made. A couple of therapy sessions earlier, Werner had asked me if I really believed he could drive a car again. I had told him then that I wanted to take him for a ride in my new car. If he wanted, he could drive. And so we went for a car ride. After six years Werner tried driving on a remote road. At first he was insecure and afraid to drive on the busy street. But I thought he could do it, and so he drove all the way home. He was a bit shaky and sweat was noticeable on his forehead when he parked the car in front of his parents' house. It was evident, however, how proud he was of managing all of this.

In the following weeks Werner rediscovered many of his own abilities. It became increasingly normal for him to leave his home everyday and run errands. He became confident and able to take credit for his accomplishments yet he was also able to admit his deficits.

Because of the progress of his healing, his family respected and valued him more. His sister and parents were proud of him. Werner's sister asked him for help with her homework. He helped her with schoolwork and preparation for exams. The acknowledgement from his family helped him to feel his own self-worth even more and his self-confidence increased.

Despite all the progress Werner was making, one giant obstacle remained and overshadowed everything else: his inability to speak. Throughout the entire therapy he had kept his compulsive thoughts. He constantly repeated the four beats of music and the words "we are" in his head. He feared that if he began to speak he would forget the music and the words—and then everything would be lost. We still communicated by writing. I asked Werner if he was able to hum a tone with his mouth closed. I did it myself and Werner copied me. We did this more often. I hummed something and Werner repeated after me. Eventually Werner practised by himself.

One day at the clinic, a year after therapy had commenced, I was called to the phone. Werner's mother was on the phone. She said Werner wanted to know if I would keep the arranged appointment with him today. "But wait a moment", she said, "someone wants to talk to you". "Hello", a voice spoke, "this is Werner. Are you coming today?" I shuddered. Werner spoke to me and I was speechless. I did not know what to say. "Hello", I heard the voice again, "are you still there or have I knocked you off your feet?" "No", I said quickly, "I am still here, but I don't know what to say—I am completely surprised."

This was the last time I went to Werner's home for therapy. From then on he came to my practice.

Consenting to a new life

Two years have passed since Werner began to speak again. During those two years Werner went to school. He successfully passed all the entry exams for school and finished the eighth grade. Next spring he will try to get the qualification necessary to leave after the tenth grade. He plans on studying social pedagogy. He has already passed that entry exam with a good grade. He now earns his money delivering pizza and he will soon move into an apartment and try to live on his own.

Therapy sessions now take place once a month. We talk about problems of daily life. Werner weighs 75 kg and plays tennis regularly. He goes to nightclubs and has met quite a few girls, some of whom would not be disinclined to begin a relationship with him. For Werner, this question is increasingly important.

Schizophrenic mental deficiency?

Even when there are many indications for such a diagnosis, we must remain critical, for it may be the most severe diagnosis a psychiatrist can give. It may eventually mean a state of irredeemable hopelessness. It may frustrate the motivation of the people involved because of the seemingly hopeless condition.

Let us remain doubtful. Even when such a diagnosis has been given, we should take a closer look and not be discouraged. Otherwise there might be a loss of life.

Reference

Längle, A. (1999). Existenzanalyse—die Zustimmung zum Leben finden. *Fundamenta Psychiatrica, 12*: 139–146.

CHAPTER NINE

The path towards inner motion: an existential-analytic psychotherapy on depression

Karin Steinert

First contact with Doris and her social background

Doris[1] wrote me an email which stated: "I am searching for my joyous spirit which I have lost somewhere. For about six years I have been suffering from depression. I have been taking medication for half a year now. The medication has at least helped me to get up in the morning and it has reduced my despair. Nonetheless, I would still like to give up on life if I could. Can you please help me? I would really like to live and view life as a great gift!" We agreed to have our first appointment together.

Doris was twenty-one years old. She had short blonde hair, wore glasses, and was slightly overweight. She looked well groomed and dressed casually, wearing large shirts and pullovers. Even in later sessions, she wore mostly beige and grey clothes. She did not wear make up. When describing her appearance, it was difficult to say anything specific about her because she appeared very inconspicuous. She did not move or exercise much and her voice sounded monotonous. Doris was polite and well adapted. She seemed particularly concerned about not doing anything that might be unpleasant to anyone.

Doris had grown up with her family in Burgenland. There were four girls in the family. She had an identical twin sister (born a couple of minutes before her) and an older and a younger sister. The parents ran a locksmith shop. Doris had gone to junior high school and then attended a college for five years. The college was a specialised school that prepared students for careers in economics—in German called *Höhere Bundeslehranstalt für wirtschaftliche Berufe* (HBLA). Doris pejoratively referred to the college as a "housekeeper's school". After attending this college she began various training programs (acting school, for example) but tended to drop out sooner or later. She had recently begun training as a physiotherapist. She was quite fond of it and had in fact stuck with it for half a year which was considered a great achievement. It was important for her to complete this training.

When therapy began Doris was living in a communal residence with two other women. She had come to know them through a Catholic women's movement. She had been actively involved in this movement but now had a very distant relationship with it. The two other women wanted to constantly talk and pray with Doris. They encouraged her to pull herself together. Doris tried to avoid them as much as possible and rarely left her room because of this.

Six months ago Doris had tried to do something about her depression for the first time. She had gone to several sessions of psychotherapy but soon stopped attending. The therapist had talked very little and had not understood or truly perceived her. Her doctor had written out a prescription for antidepressants. This had helped her to get up in the morning and attend school. She hoped therapy would provide support, new encounters, and skills for daily life.

Attending school: the beginning of depression

Doris described herself as a lively and interested child. She also did well when she attended secondary school. When she encountered injustice, she had the feeling that she could (and was encouraged to) defend herself.

When Doris attended college at the HBLA, she felt truly bad for the first time. When therapy began she told me that one particular teacher had often ignored her and treated her unfairly. When she talked about this with him, he simply made pejorative statements or sanctioned her with punishments. Doris even changed college. She attended a different HBLA college at another location. At the new college she again felt powerless and helpless. At that point she decided for herself that it would be better for her not to say anything at all anymore, to be silent, to simply swallow all the experienced and felt injustices, in order to draw as little attention to herself as possible and get these years of school over with in any way possible.

When Doris was seventeen she went on a three-year practicum as part of her HBLA studies. She went to an island in the north of Germany and experienced extreme rejection there. She worked as a waitress and was treated very badly by her female boss. Here, again, she had the feeling of not being able to defend herself, of not being allowed to be. Doris tried to evade the attacks perpetrated by her boss by working harder than the others. She got up earlier and worked seven days a week. But her boss continued to put her down and told her that she was an impossible person. After three months Doris became unsure whether she did not in fact deserve this bad treatment.

When therapy began, Doris talked about her experiences at the HBLA. She could not understand what had caused her to sink into such deep resignation. She had been a strong person prior to this. The various stories she told were all disconnected pieces of a picture and could not be connected in a meaningful way. It was only after many therapy sessions, sessions that focused on her time at school and viewed it from alternate perspectives, that I could detect a connected meaning.

Doris told me (much later in therapy) that she had always wanted to be an actress, but in order to attend acting school one had to be seventeen. Her twin sister had attended an art school while Doris went on to attend the HBLA. After a couple of weeks Doris had realised that the school was not for her. The content did not interest her at all. Her family nevertheless encouraged her to continue with her studies there and graduate with a "useful" degree. Doris often had to defend herself against the attacks of the teachers but she could not change her situation, being at a school that did not interest her. Changing schools did not improve her well-being very much. The new school was of the same type. She felt increasingly tired and lacked energy. In addition, she started eating a lot and quickly gained weight. This had a negative effect upon her self-worth. Doris was under extreme pressure to get through her five years of school. During this time she lost herself and drifted off into passiveness, which ultimately led to a depression.

The relationship to oneself and the world

It was more than two years after graduating from the HBLA before Doris went to therapy. Her depressive symptoms had not gone away after graduation. For five years Doris had disregarded her own needs and, as a result, lost the relationship to herself and to the things she considered important. She had disregarded herself in order to bear the burdening situations at school. Even after her graduation and the change in outer circumstances, it was impossible for Doris to reconstruct a positive relationship to herself, because for a long time she had not played any significant role in her own life. She had lost a sense for her own wishes and needs because she constantly put herself last. She had increasingly lost a sense of her own worth. Due to this, her readiness to internalise others' negative opinions of her grew, and she subsequently adopted these same opinions of herself as well. She once told me: "I was present at an accident once. The most important thing was that everyone else was doing well. That was my primary concern. Not until after that did I take a look at myself to see how I was doing." Doris considered her own life to be worthless. The demands and the well-being of others were always more important than her own.

Doris was also no longer in tune with her own emotions because she paid no attention to her needs. She no longer knew or felt which direction to go in. She did not know what she liked or what she needed. She had created a construct of ideas about herself and the world and tried to find an orientation from it.

Only in a later phase of therapy could Doris accurately describe her condition. When she got up in the morning, she already had very clear notions and concepts about what was supposed to happen that day and how she should behave. This construct provided security, guidance, and safety. She therefore did not have to constantly decide what she would or would not do. She did not have to repeatedly try to sense in which direction to go at a given point in time. Using her construct she moved ahead step by step. Yet the motivation for this movement did not come from an inner motivation, but the result of an imposed set of rules. Her construct was extremely inflexible and stiff. It imprisoned her and left no room for inner (only for outer) movement. There was always the danger of getting stuck because she lacked this inner motivation.

When Doris tried to implement her conceptions and expectations about herself, she was very strict. She sometimes lay in bed, for example, and listened to the radio. She told herself that this type of behaviour was much too lazy and that she should sit at the table and drink tea instead. She had high expectations for herself and quickly arrived at an attitude of devaluation ("too lazy") when she did not conform to her own imposed conceptions.

Doris also found it extremely hard to say "no" if others asked her for something or asked her to do something. She did not say "no" even when she knew that she did not have sufficient time and that it would be too much for her. To resolve this kind of conflict a person would have to have a clear and firm attitude. Since Doris felt she did not possess this attitude, she tried to avoid people and situations like these. She did not feel valuable and was in danger of giving herself up for others. She could not turn down the demands of others because it made her feel like she was someone—it made her feel valuable.

Doris visited her family at home in Burgenland every weekend. There were tensions at home with her twin sister. Doris often compared herself to her sister. According to Doris, her sister was much more attractive and had a better looking body. She felt her sister was more interesting to other people. Doris admired her sister and wanted to be as calm and laidback as she was. Doris often sewed dresses for her twin sister but not for herself as she thought that she would have to lose weight before wearing such attractive clothes. Doris remembered that she had felt slightly better when her sister had gone to the United States for a couple of weeks. She had felt almost liberated at the time. The comparison to her sister was a constant burden.

Much later in therapy (sometime around the twentieth session) Doris told me that as a child she had had the opinion that, "It would be enough if one of us made it." If one of the sisters received a good grade on an exam, for example, the grade of the other was not as important. There had been a certain balance during high school. They took turns getting good grades. But after her sister had gone to art school and Doris had "only" attended a "housekeeper's school", everything became clear to Doris: her sister had "made it" while she received the leftover, "worthless junk".

The suicidal crisis

When the first sunny days of spring arrived, Doris plunged into a great crisis. She wrote an email to me expressing her despair:

> For the last two days I have felt as if I was alone in this world. There is nothing meaningful in this world which would make me want to live. I see flowers, the sun, laughing people, but I cannot understand it; I can't see it—it means nothing to me. I am so sorry. I love my family and I do not want to cause trouble for anyone. Is everything somehow not my fault because I am this way?

We made an appointment for that same day.

Doris was extremely desperate when she arrived at her therapy session. She should have been in school but she did not want to go. When I asked her repeatedly if something had happened that had made her feel desperate, she said that she could not think of anything specific. This would turn out to be false. Prior to the crisis she had written an email to a friend. She had contacted him and opened herself up. Her friend had ended their correspondence after a few days and did not write to her again. Doris felt rejected and worthless. She believed it was her "fault" that he broke off the correspondence, although she did not explore the real reasons for his reaction. "He betrayed me and won't write to me again," she said. "And that is not surprising. Nobody is really interested in me. I am boring and uninteresting. Everything is completely my fault. With things the way they are I don't want any relationship whatsoever!" Yet at the same time, Doris was demanding of herself not to be affected by "such a minor event". She thought that she must "transcend" such an incident, that it was really "nothing" to her. On the one hand, she had been touched, but she did not want to feel that something was wrong. On account of this mindset, she avoided any affection and steered herself into a dead end. Here she came to a complete inner standstill where there was no possibility of escape. She felt that the only option left was suicide.

In this acute crisis situation it was impossible for Doris to see the overarching connections. She desired nothing anymore and everything seemed meaningless to her. She just wanted to be left alone and to do nothing. She thought often of committing suicide by slitting her wrists.

She even feared not being able to control herself anymore and actually acting upon her thoughts. Doris could not handle being alone in her apartment in Vienna and she did not want to be at school either. She thought it would be better to be at home in Burgenland with her family but she did not want to burden them. Her family home also seemed very far away and difficult to get to in her condition. In addition, her family had planned to go on vacation in a couple of days and she would then have been all alone at the house. She did not want this either. I asked her if she would consider going to a hospital for a couple of days. Doris was relieved to hear this option. We also talked about her mother picking her up and taking her to the hospital. She would like this best. But she was shy about calling her mother and asking her because she did not want to be a burden to her.

At this point Doris knew fairly accurately what she needed but disregarded her needs because she did "not want to be a burden to anyone". In this situation I took control and told Doris that it was not about burdening anyone at the moment but about preserving and protecting her life. By taking this position, I implicitly told her that it was common sense to survive and that I would support her unconditionally. Doris sensed that I would not leave her alone and that I was close to her. I let her be as she was in this moment. I did not try to change her. Her life was the primary concern at that moment. A present and engaged therapeutic relationship such as this can lead to consciousness and from this consciousness a future may develop for the patient. Space opens up which may lead to a path.

During this particular therapy session Doris called her mother in Burgenland and asked her to pick her up directly from my practice in Vienna and take her to the hospital. Her mother agreed immediately and came to pick her up. Doris then spent the night at a psychiatric hospital. Her stay there was not a relief, however, but an extreme deprivation of her independence. None of the doctors took her seriously and she spent the night in an emergency bed in the hallway. Nevertheless, Doris reached a decisive turning point during that night. Doris described it at a later date as follows: "I was lying awake during the night in the hospital. I could not sleep. I truly felt that I had reached rock bottom. Until then I had always had the sensation of falling, but now I had reached the bottom. It could not get any worse than this, but from this point on, things could only improve." She also said: "In this situation of complete deprivation I sensed very clearly that I did not want to give up on my life. I sensed that I liked to live!" Later Doris said that although it was difficult, she would not have wanted to miss out on this experience. It became a foundation for her and she did not doubt this foundation in the sessions that followed. It marked the first step towards an inner motion.

The path towards inner motion

When Doris reached "rock bottom", she felt alive. At this point she decided to live. It became the starting point for all further activities. After this incident Doris began to take care of herself and to slowly reconstruct a relationship to herself. Of course it was not the last time she was confronted with devaluing situations and dead ends, but now she did not remain in a state of hopelessness. She took herself by the hand and sought out a path. But how had Doris managed to get to this point?

A decisive factor was certainly the relationship between us, the relationship established during therapy. My attitude towards her, the patient, had been emphatic and welcoming. This meant that I approached Doris in her world and offered a present and understanding relationship. I invested myself. At the beginning of therapy I was the one who was actively involved in the relationship. This was an attitude that was extremely necessary for Doris in her depressed mood. It was also the reason why Doris had not felt comfortable going to her former therapist who hardly talked at all and could not be felt by her. It was my goal to lead the patient to a good and improved relationship to herself and to her world.

A depressive experience occurs when every possible path for movement is blocked, when there is no apparent way to escape from a dead end. It occurs when a person has the feeling of being caught in a web of powerlessness. As a therapist, I took Doris by the hand—metaphorically speaking—and led her. I stayed on the path with her and did not leave her. On account of this, a path towards inner motion was opened up for her. Inner motion and inner response became possible and acceptable to her. Of course, there was also the fear of opening up.

Doris went on to make a pivotal breakthrough in a later phase of therapy. She ventured forward in order to break through the tight corset of her own expectations. On one occasion we discussed the option of Doris taking an hour once in a while and not planning anything during that time. She could then sense what she would like to do and act upon it. Doris was terribly afraid of this because she thought it would trigger her intemperate eating habit if she just let herself go and gave up control. Nonetheless, she found courage to do this one afternoon. It was essential for her to promise that she would not condemn herself afterwards, no matter how much she ate or what else happened. After Doris consciously made the decision to go through with the experiment of following her inner motion, she did not have the immediate desire to eat. On the contrary, her extreme desire for food weakened and she experienced her time with vitality. She did not feel tired and was able to try things out. She watched shows on TV which she normally did not ("because they are too stupid"). She baked cookies for her family and rode her bicycle in the evening, something she had not done in a long time. She experienced liveliness and nothing terrible happened when she trusted her inner sense. This experience was a further step in coming into contact with her inner motion and acting upon it. She lost her fear and distrust of herself, again, something that had only hindered her. On account of this newfound trust she could let her inner motion affect her and remain close to herself.

A perspective for the future

Doris' therapy has yet to come to a conclusion but the sessions now take place once a month. They serve mainly as a support and an opportunity to talk about situations in which Doris still experiences herself as a prisoner. In the meantime, Doris has established such a good inner relationship to herself that she can take care of herself without constant instruction from someone else.

Both her relationship with herself and her environment have changed. She has moved out of the apartment she shared, and did not like, and now lives with her family in Burgenland. Although she has to commute to Vienna every day, she feels very much at home and is able to stand by her decision ("although a twenty-one-year-old should not live with her parents anymore"). Doris meets up with her friends more often and deals more effectively with her difficult relationship with her twin sister.

Doris has activated her inner motion again and is able to follow this feeling. She knows about the dangers, the specific expressions and appearances of the depressive retreat. But, when she comes to that point, she is able to activate her inner motion and get back into contact with herself and her world.

Note

1. Names and dates, which could lead to the identification of the person, have been changed.

CHAPTER TEN

" … And after a suicide attempt I have to keep on living!"

Rupert Dinhobl

"You have hindered me from doing the only egoistical thing in my life. You have sentenced me, even condemned me to live!" This quote is not from a French existential author but from a woman named Karin. While staying in a dormitory for crisis intervention and suicide prevention, Karin greeted me with this statement. I was supposed to supply psychotherapeutic care for her.

Karin was an attractive forty-four-year-old woman. She gave an initial impression of being a determined, strong, even aggressive woman. When I met her, a male nurse was busy calming her down. Karin had tried to break a window, twisting her arm to do so. "I cannot stand to be locked up like this. I need freedom and fresh air." Quite quickly we established our first contact. When I offered my psychotherapeutic assistance, she said: "If you believe that there is any use in that, let's do it." From the entry registration I gathered that Karin had tried to poison herself by taking a high, potentially lethal dose of asthma medication. As a result she had been comatose for several hours and had suffered from an organic psycho-syndrome of the brain. She was disoriented about time and place. Later on she was diagnosed with a lesion to the hippocampus which greatly decreased her memory, especially her short-term memory. She had also gone through an episode of deep depression, yet without showing any symptoms of psychosis.

Karin had had a negative mindset throughout her two-year stay at the hospital. At first she had been admitted full-time, staying day and night. She then came during the day and, finally, she was treated as an outpatient. In reference to her suicide attempt, she said: "Why did my daughter have to find me? It was my fault. I should have stayed in my bedroom after taking the pills. I wanted to die and now I have been coerced into living out my completely meaningless life."

During Karin's stay at the hospital she talked more and more about her life and the experiences she had had. Her husband, for whom she had also worked full-time, had been a carpenter. She drove trucks for him, unloaded many heavy goods, did the books for the company, and took care of her husband as well as her young daughter. She did the housekeeping on the side. There had been a collapse five years ago, when her husband had suffered a deadly accident. Two further losses destroyed everything that was meaningful in Karin's life: the loss of her boyfriend, and the "loss" of her daughter.

When I met Karin, her daughter Mary was twenty years old. When Mary entered her professional life, Karin decided that her daughter did not need her mother anymore. This, of course, was Karin's view of the issue. Mary also began dating a new boyfriend at the time. In addition to the problems with her daughter, Karin's own boyfriend had left her. Part of the reason for this was Karin's daughter. Mary had not accepted him. "My life is now meaningless and empty. There is no one who I can take care of," she said. Karin lacked the classic "purpose in life"; it had been buried. Her ability to transcend herself was also blocked, and on account of this the fourth fundamental motivation (see Chapter Three) had caved in.

In this depressive phase (second fundamental motivation) Karin *sensed* that she had lost her perspective in life, the "purpose of life". After the loss of her husband she had "become a husband to herself": she was strict with herself, demanded clarity, truthfulness, and justice. These were the fundamental virtues of her philosophy. Karin had never been able to ask herself in childhood "What do I *like*?" She had not done this in her later life either. She had to function. During her childhood she had been a mediator between her half bothers and her father. Later on she had to function as part of her husband's family. After his death she had to provide an existence for her daughter who was still a child.

She did not even have enough time to grieve for her husband. The consequence of this was a serious depression. Her answer to the question of the second fundamental motivation is therefore not surprising. When she was asked if she had liked to live prior to her suicide attempt, her answer was: "Zero—nothing. I just did not *like* to live anymore."

But who exactly *was* Karin? (This is the question of the third fundamental motivation.) She came across as a strong, powerful woman, who had also never learned to listen to the voice inside of herself. Life had never been about *sensing* her feelings. "Throughout my entire lifetime I have never been asked what I wanted for myself." For a time her father had served in the military. He wanted to raise her in his own way, the way that he thought best. Open opposition was useless. As a result, Karin had hardened on the inside. When he locked her up inside the house so that she would eat her food, she threw it out the window one spoonful at a time. Later in life, anyone who made enemies with her was in serious trouble and women were especially at risk. As a consequence, she was consistently and relentlessly rejected. Her favourite colours were black and white and she dressed in these colors. Her world view was also black and white. She was trained as a technical draughtswoman, and her biography was also characterised by straight lines. She could not tolerate any deviance from her black and white viewpoint. Anything fancy or extravagant was unbearable to her.

In essence, Karin's development could be understood as follows. The death of her husband had caused her expectations for life to break down. She lost her meaning in life when her daughter became independent and her boyfriend left her (fourth fundamental motivation). Yet her life motto had always been, "Stay strong, keep on going, function well, and settle everything by yourself" (This demonstrated Karin's lack of reference to other people, becoming a person *through* and *with* other people. This refers to the third fundamental motivation). At this point she did not consult professional help. Karin experienced a cessation of present, inner liveliness within herself and a breakdown of dialogue with the outside world. Her inner dialogue had long been at a standstill and she had merely functioned, disregarding her inner self. Karin lost her openness towards her own emotionality. Because she lacked contact with her own liveliness, she descended deeper and deeper into a depressive development (second fundamental motivation). This was a visible warning sign. But Karin was an "all or nothing" woman and, because of this, the only option that remained open to her was suicide. All her life she had found security within herself. Yet at this point her strategy for handling life was no longer sufficient. The fateful events of her life had shaken her security in the world and her confidence in her own abilities. Here, the loss of the first fundamental motivation became evident. *Karin's development could be seen as a cascading collapse of the four fundamental motivations of existence.* This eventually led to the mindset of "I do not want to live anymore". At the time of the suicide attempt, Karin's liveliness had already been severely reduced. Therefore, the desire to put an end to her life was quite present.

As stated, Karin's suicidal development could be seen as a *cascading collapse of the four fundamental motivations.* Therapy was therefore an attempt to *reconstruct the four fundamental motivations step by step and layer by layer.* The foundation for reconstruction was finding strength to endure the difficult and almost hopeless situation. Life at this stage was about enduring the situation and being able to simply be there (first fundamental motivation). This was also true when Karin's negativity was coupled with verbal and passive aggression. A renewed attitude of "being there" and also of "being with someone"—experienced in (through) therapy—softened her hardness and bitterness to some degree. During the course of therapy the loss of her job as well as the cessation of friendships became further testing points. The unexpected commencement of her daughter's studies was also a test for Karin. Her daughter now lived with her boyfriend close to the university. Yet the growing awareness that she was not capable of working anymore proved to be the greatest challenge for Karin. The fact that her capacity for memory was greatly reduced prohibited her from going back to work. As a result, Karin had to apply for an early pension. This was particularly difficult because work had always meant so much to her.

Karin was able to soften her negative attitude to some degree by being able to finally grieve the death of her husband (second fundamental motivation). Karin was now able to cry and this softened her facial contours. Yet this was not the substantial breakthrough for her. She was still continuously suicidal and latently aggressive. This was often difficult for us (the treatment team, consisting of a female doctor, therapists, and nurses) to handle. Karin reached a decisive turning point when she was confronted with her negative attitude towards life. We tried to speak to Karin personally (third fundamental motivation). We clearly explained that the process of therapy would only lead to a meaningful path if she *assisted* us. We could only *work together* and not against each other. We told her: "It is pointless if we pull on one end of the rope and you on the other. Shall we not go in the direction of life together?" She basically agreed to this. By asking further questions on this matter her decision was increasingly confirmed. The next question to address was *how* she was to reach this goal. While exploring this issue did not lead to concrete results, our confrontation with her did affect the course of treatment and there was a noticeable turn for the better. The shell that Karin had constructed around herself crumbled more and more. Sometimes Karin smiled and from time to time she even made jokes—she obviously had a very dry sense of humour.

Two years after Karin's suicide attempt (in her case the term "failed suicide" would be more appropriate) she is able to live in her own apartment. She has a strong connection with a friend who is also part of a group of pub friends. Her mood has stabilised and Karin attends a therapy session once a month. Yet Karin has not found a stable perspective on life (in the sense of the fourth fundamental motivation). She says: "I am too stupid to kill myself. But now I can at least take advantage of the welfare system. I have paid long enough for it during my working days!" But she also says: "I want to enjoy life as much as possible. I go to the coffee house and read the paper there quite frequently. That's alright because I forget most of it anyway. That way I never get bored." But tears still stream down her face when she revisits her "wounds". "There are things that I have not discussed with anyone yet and I do not want to either." We have not gone into these issues, yet. The big question remains whether her attitude is sufficient enough for life (or even for survival). We will continue to accompany Karin further.

CHAPTER ELEVEN

"After all, only dumb people can be happy": narcissistic personalities

Liselotte Tutsch

Taking a first look

Mr. A. began attending therapy because, according to him, he had problems with his hysterical girlfriend. He was willing to marry her but she tried to evade the matter, beating around the bush by keeping him out of her life and away from her children from a previous marriage. To him this was quite obviously a sign of her hysterical mindset. He had offered her almost everything that she could possibly desire, but she hardly appreciated it.

He was a surgeon and somewhat under pressure because he had applied for a management position in a hospital and been rejected twice. "Oh well, all of these envious schemers. I should not let it bother me in the least," Mr. A. told me. At times, he confessed, he did have real feelings of hatred for these people.

He casually asked me to address him from the left side, since he was almost deaf in his right ear and my voice was indeed a bit too quiet. He also told me that his left eye was extremely shortsighted; he was almost blind in that eye. I thought that this might have been the reason why he had come to my practice and I asked him if this affected his operating skills in any way. "No problem at all," he answered shortly.

Instead of addressing this matter further, he talked about the beautiful mansion that he had bought for his future family. He also talked about his professional career: "My colleagues are just so incompetent." About his mother he said that he was the most precious thing in the world to her. She really had nothing else except him. When I asked if this posed a problem for him in anyway, he said: "No, not at all. Nothing to worry about!"

Despite his attitude, he had in fact done something that was not alright. He had hit his girlfriend—his hand had "slipped". In a way this had shocked him, but he stated that she had also been very hysterical. He stated further that this would of course never happen again! "After a couple of sessions I should be able to control myself. What do you think?" According to Mr. A. his girlfriend was the one who needed therapy, but he would do it. This was no problem for him.

"If you need this time slot in order to attend to someone else, you can cancel our appointment," he told me in good humour as he left.

This short dialogue with Mr. A. already reveals the essentials of a narcissistic dysfunction. Narcissistic people lack the inner ability to identify a problem and perceive the dysfunction to be external. They emphasise their own competence and greatness while their behaviour within relationships is inappropriate.

The case of Mr. B. was quite different. He attended the therapy session because—so he told me—his secretary thought he needed to work on himself. When I asked him what he needed to work on, he did not answer. He also gave no reply when I asked him what *he* thought about attending therapy. After exerting a great effort to discover symptoms of some kind, I was almost relieved to diagnose a mild fear of flying in him. Mr. B. asserted, though, that this fear was "probably due to a labile sense of balance". Therefore it wasn't really a topic to discuss in therapy. He did have a fairly developed phobia of spiders. "But what does it matter?" he said, "It's not like I live out in the jungle." Eventually he did tell me that he was not doing well generally. He said he always felt bad yet qualified this by saying, "After all, there isn't anything truly good about the world and life anyway." Yes, he felt somewhat depressed. In fact, he did not want to change; he just wanted to live in peace. He wanted to sit anonymously in the lobby of some magnificent hotel amidst the people walking about or to be on a giant cruise ship and sail the seas. Unfortunately, he did not earn enough money to afford this kind of lifestyle.

What the client asked of me

Mr. B. desired nothing in particular. Perhaps he wanted me to alleviate his depressive mood, although he believed that it really could not be changed. He told me that it had always been that way for him. Perhaps he simply wanted someone else to pay him attention and yet ask nothing of him. He liked that sort of thing. I stated that it was up to him if he were to get something useful from our talks. I suggested that our first task should be a unified attempt to identify certain themes and issues that we could then discuss. "Yes, that seems to be a good idea. An hour per week, at a fixed time. Then I can still read the paper at the cafe later on." Did he like going to the cafe? "No, it's boring." Why did he go then? "It's perhaps a bit less boring than most of the other stuff."

It was only during later sessions that he confessed why he had truly come to therapy. Although he had increasingly gained control over and distanced himself from everything that went on, he had flashes of anger which were quite embarrassing to him—"Something like that should not happen!" Being on top of things and in total control were of the utmost importance for him. In fact, he preferred to have no contact with people rather than lose his superiority, for this would be *embarrassing*.

Mr. B. wanted nothing in particular of me. He just wanted me to "think about" his person and "ask questions" about him. What he got out of this kind of interaction he did not tell me for a long time.

This case study reveals further narcissistic phenomena. Being in the presence of a narcissistic person is both a puzzle and meaningful. He seems *untouchable* and *diffuse* when it comes to experiencing himself and the world. Every experience of the narcissistic person places him into a pre-personal condition in which he presents himself to the world.

An "open" or a "hidden" form of narcissism?

These two cases reveal various manifestations of narcissism. Mr. A. was "openly" narcissistic. He belongs to the "loud", exhibitionist type, who glorifies himself and *demands* confirmation from others. If there is anything that decreases his grandeur, he only mentions it on the side. It does not even seem to enter his consciousness as a problem.

Mr. B., on the other hand, belongs to the quiet, somewhat autistic type. His grandeur, which is puzzling and untouchable, does not demand any explanatory words. Perhaps there are no words to truly describe his grandeur. His life is so close to the "centre of perfection" that it can only remain that way if he keeps his distance from other people and refrains from contact. If his oceanic harmony is ever disturbed, he suffers self-doubt and feelings of insecurity. The quiet type finds stability in maintaining distance from others. Such people imagine themselves to be perfect. Either this or they are very cultured. They want other people to see them as "a very strange character" or as "a person the likes of whom no one has seen before". They ask the therapist questions like: "I bet you have never had a fool like me in therapy?"

A main characteristic of the narcissistic person is a lack of relationships in life, a lack of openness and a lack of empathy towards others. These characteristics reveal themselves in antisocial tendencies. They exist in both forms of manifestation.

Taking a closer look

While talking with Mr. A. and Mr. B., I noticed that they only experienced the world self-referentially. As such, only the client's contribution to the interaction is of importance; everyone else's viewpoint remains veiled and unessential. Although the narcissistic person has an air of grandeur and tries to impress people, conversations with him may often lead to boredom and emptiness. Entire conversations revolve around the narcissistic person who is looking for applause and success. Even if the narcissistic person is highly intelligent, he has the tendency to use commonplace statements. Most of the time there is no dialogue. When the narcissistic person has explained everything on his mind, the talk often ends with a statement like, "What a pleasant talk that was." The charming and childlike impression he exudes does not compensate for his lack of humour (the use of humour and irony, an opposite of superiority, and the ability to laugh about oneself are not strengths of the narcissistic person). He will often make pejorative statements like, "Only dumb people can really be happy." While he *appears* to be in excellent spirits, he can cause a sombre mood among people and is unable to disperse the omnipresent emptiness.

"Concerning other people ..."

A narcissistic person lacks the feeling for appropriate behaviour in social situations. This often leads to embarrassing and insinuating situations.

For example, Mr. F., another client, observed me closely without any sense of shame. He seemed very interested in the fact that I was wearing socks with my jeans. He appeared to have no feeling regarding the inappropriateness and lack of distance towards me implied in his statement. When I asked him why this concerned him, he replied again, quite inappropriately: "Well, my wife finds socks like that somewhat impossible. I will tell her she might be wrong in this matter." The client lacked empathy and talked in an invading manner. He emphasised the significance of the therapist without stating his own opinion. Behaviour like this often causes the communicating partner to feel annoyed on account of the insinuating statement and "proud" owing to the importance attached to him.

The narcissistic mode of relationship is even evident in physical behaviour. A narcissistic person may stand on her toes, shove someone aside, and make room for herself with no regard to the other person. She acts as if the other person does not even exist. On the other hand, a narcissistic person may act gallantly and conscientiously. She tends to switch back and forth between these opposite forms of behaviour.

She sees the other person mainly as a "provider" (Kernberg, 1988). The narcissistic person is ambitious, even greedy when it comes to consuming anything from her environment that may reflect and confirm her. Yet, she can also "destroy" anything that is critical and separates her from this confirmation. She may view the other person as an ideal in order to be part of something great. Or she may deny the other person his individuality in order to achieve her purpose with him. The other person will first enjoy the attention given to him, but then quickly feel misused. The narcissist makes a person feel like he is merely an object for self-preservation.

The narcissistic person has a promiscuous tendency, which expresses itself in a lack of relationships, an addiction to confirmation, and an inner vacancy. A person like this demands a variety of experiences, both numerous and highly appealing to the senses.

Living in the eternal present

Although the narcissistic greed is focused on reception, the satisfaction derived from attention, success, and applause soon vanishes. The achievements soon fade and a vacant feeling takes over. Experiences hardly make an impression because the narcissist lives her life in the *eternal present.* "The glorified self remains alone and exists in a strange, timeless world of repetitive cycles, made up of wishes, temporary idealization, greedy consumption and vanishing resources due to destruction, disappointment and devaluation". The passing of time and the aging process creates an overwhelming situation for the narcissist. Such a person is "unprepared for the change that occurs with time" (Kernberg, 1988, p. 156).

The narcissist lives from one moment to the next. She extracts confirmation of her perfection from whatever situation she is in, sucking it dry "like a vampire". Her experience does not conquer with reality, though, so her past does not provide a stable history for her.

According to my careful hypothesis, the lack of history manifests itself "neurologically": a narcissistic person easily forgets and suffers from an increasing and rapid "progression" of dementia.

Pseudo-juvenile behaviour

The lack of a stable history coupled with an inner vacancy often reveals itself through continuous juvenile behaviour. Time seems to have no effect upon the person. He does not recognise different ages, for example, and his own physical aging goes unnoticed.

Mr. D., for example, considered it an insult when his wife, "looking the way she does", thought it possible he was still interested in her. Yet, Mr. D. was by no means handsome himself. Therefore, his curious statement was even more embarrassing.

Pseudo-dependency

The narcissist's reference to his grandeur often gives the impression of *pseudo-dependency*. He lives with the feeling of not needing anyone. The world is in fact much more at a loss if *he* does not "grace it with his presence".

When the "intake" is blocked, however, boredom and vacancy come to the surface. These are the expressions of the vacuum that veils the deep fear of meaninglessness and the pain of the early insult the narcissist received.

Mr. A. was in a miserable state when his partner left him. When I asked him how he felt, his whining attitude changed to a cool, nonchalant facade. "Actually, you know, I am not too sad about her being gone.

But she was quite beautiful and everyone envied me. I know it's bad to say that," he told me with an air of pride.

"Bad things always occur from outside," or, "It is always the other's fault"

The narcissistic person lets nothing contaminate the view she has of herself. Therefore, anything unpleasant or any failure is always seen as the other person's fault. Yet if her own failure is clearly evident, then her anger and rage turn into narcissistic self-destruction (Narcissistic self-destruction expresses itself in annihilating self-accusations, in devaluing the self, and thinking oneself to be completely incapable).

No applause, no accomplishments

The narcissistic regime even reigns supreme in the field of accomplishments. Taking interest in a subject is secondary. How an accomplishment is *received* is far more important. The narcissist is therefore only capable of accomplishing something if the environment applauds her. Otherwise she is disabled by blocks, and lacks joy and motivation.

Often, a narcissist will overvalue her own abilities. She will often speak of great accomplishments which are only partly rooted in reality. Common experiences are emphasised and blown out of proportion, for example.

Morals without ethics

Another evident characteristic is the discrepancy between the idealisation of a noble system of values and principles, and an outgrowth of antisocial tendencies. The narcissist has her *own morals*. She is full of ideals and principles, but otherwise without personal ethics. She holds fast to primitive ideals and constructs a code of honour that becomes hypocritical.

Hate and envy

The narcissist's inner experience of insult quickly evokes feelings of hate. The inner feeling of annihilation motivates the narcissist to annihilate someone or something. Anyone who is different or even better will soon be the enemy. He is envious of anyone who receives more recognition, attention or success. This is the result of a greatly threatened self-esteem. If the narcissist cannot be the best, then he is the worst; he is nothing at all.

Worthless grandeur

Due to selective self-reference and an undifferentiated experience of the world, the narcissist loses a system of values and has no interest in anything other than his own grandeur. The narcissist can therefore only speak from within the tight confinement of commonplace statements and generalisations. This general terminology ("everything, never, nothing, one ..."), coupled with feelings of inner emptiness and nothingness, is a sign of narcissistic development.

Behind the veil of appearance: neediness and fear

Narcissists put up a front of obtrusiveness and untouchable distance. Behind this front they often appear lovable, naive, needy, and more or less openly dependent on the reactions of other people.

Mr. A., for example, waited after every sentence for a sign of recognition on my part. In truth he was not interested in extensive, complimentary, or differentiating remarks. He disregarded or devalued them. He needed *confirmation* in order to feel well. He was not able to formulate needs or wishes. He once called me between appointments and told me that he had come out of an operation early and asked if I was perhaps in the mood to have a little therapy session. The tone of his voice was not obtrusive. He spoke with a strange tone of normality. When I listened more closely, I could hear that he was very concerned about concealing his need for help and his fear of rejection. "Oh, you can't? Well, that's ok. It's nothing urgent; it would just be on the way for me. Just perhaps a short question, since we're talking already ... my girlfriend broke up with me yesterday ..."

Mr. B.'s situation was quite different. He concealed his neediness even more. On one occasion when he arrived late, as usual, I used the extra time to collect my mail. I therefore did not open the door immediately. I could see him through the glass window of the door. He did not see me approaching. I could see fear, even panic in his face. He was literally falling apart at the seams; he seemed to be dissolving, and rang the doorbell several times with increasing intensity. When I opened the door, he jumped, caught himself and then, when he looked at the mail, said in his usual distant manner: "You receive an unusually large amount of mail. You must be an important woman!" It gave him an obvious sense of satisfaction and joy to have "such an important" therapist. This completely restored him. His neediness, fear, and apparent weakness were concealed from others and from himself as well. He did not admit to it.

Keeping up the "narcissistic balance"

The "technique" of keeping up the narcissistic balance is an inner and outer *intolerance to difference*. Manifestations of this are:

1. an addiction to harmony;
2. a hunger for confirmation;
3. a life untouched and protected by distance.

The "narcissistic warning system" is activated when this balance is threatened. The warning system consists of:

– hypochondriasis (the somatic equivalent of intolerance for difference; it is the exaggerated state of physical alertness or sensation to physical disruption);
– an extreme sensitivity to critique;
– hate towards anything disruptive;
– a form of depression that covers everything painful in emotional numbness.

The fragility of these efforts is evident. The construct easily collapses and imperfection breaks through. There is an inner emotional numbness and emptiness. A narcissistic person feels the constant nag of self-doubt when questioned. This, in turn, leads to a renewed, hectic search for balance and satisfaction. Behaviour like this shuts life out. The ego is blocked and the person cannot experience herself in her life.

The narcissist is unable to take a position and implement values. She lacks a "bridge" towards existence. There is no "you", there is only an "object" and no personal development.

How does this come about?

Considerations on the etiology of the pathology

The narcissistic self, with its affinity to grandeur, is constantly threatened by nothingness. In my view, besides the important dispositions of narcissism, there are three typical fundamental constellations of the psychological genesis. Narcissism is created by a violent destruction or a "gentle smothering" of imperfect parts of a personality. These parts are dissociated. They threaten the self-worth of a person when they are "awakened" by critique from the outside.

The "tragic threefold constellation for narcissism" is common and fundamental to the disorder:

1. a pejorative, annihilating, negative, and mocking critique; it is often accompanied by a comparison to an idealised role model;
2. insecurity caused by uncritical glorification and denial of all weaknesses;
3. keeping the painful experiences of the world out of a symbiotic relationship with a mostly depressed, unhappy mother (Parsifal syndrome); the mother wants to create a more wholesome world and does not realise the problems and conflicts of the child, or does not let them surface in the first place.

Mocking, glorification or possessive spoiling of a child can lead to a fragile feeling of self-worth. The view the child then has of himself shifts to a pole of grandeur. The development of the self only permits perfection. Imperfection, ordinariness, and suffering are not allowed to enter. This is how a rigid identity of pretense is formed and is very sensitive to even minimal disturbances. The narcissist finds it increasingly difficult to keep up this facade owing to the fact that as he gets older, he loses his vitality and social possibilities. The dissociated parts of the personality continually attack the self-worth of the person but use the critique of others as a cover. This leads to increasingly intense and helpless efforts of compensation, which in older age often leads to deep depression, bitterness, or a socially desolate condition.

Fundamental approaches of therapy

"Basso Continuo" of therapy: a basic attitude of taking the person seriously and valuing them

Therapy consists of supplying the fundamental needs of a person (Längle, 1992). These are: the need for protection, space, and security;

for relationship, time, closeness, and empathy; for respect and to be valued; and, finally, for openness and meaning. Therapy supplies these needs with varying priority and importance depending on the necessity and condition of the patient.

The narcissistic disturbance calls for the discovery of the self and the self-worth of the patient. Taking the patient seriously, valuing, and respecting her will lead to a promotion of self-worth. The therapist also needs to pay attention to the seemingly unimportant things in life, the quiet tones. At the beginning, therapy should provide a slightly "narcissistic colouring" to the dialogue in order to bring about the willingness for argument and dialogue within the patient. For example, respect needs an air of high respect; valuing needs an air of glorification; confrontation needs an honouring undertone; and anything that is merely average needs a match in significance.

The attitude that characterises the therapeutic relationship provides the frame and precondition for the narcissist to begin a relationship with herself. It is the foundation for the late maturing process.

"There is no one around"—how should we begin?

In order to bring the patient into a motion of change, therapy should promote a resource-oriented expansion of her abilities. It must do this without attacking the defensive structures (Kohut, 1976) or working against them.

In my view, the first phase of therapy with narcissistic patients consists of three fundamental motions:

a. searching for the person beyond the narcissistic defense and creating a possibility for relationship;
b. accepting defensive structures, bearing, and relieving them;
c. strengthening compensational structures, expanding and promoting abilities.

a) Searching for the person

The searching phase is a challenge because the narcissist is merely looking for an atmospheric confirmation of his personhood. He is looking for an echo. Finding a theme and commencing a dialogue can be difficult for him. Due to the inner emptiness of the patient, it is difficult to have a discussion with real content.

During the first year of therapy with Mr. B., the sessions were always similar: Mr. B. arrived at the last minute or was late, shook my hand with half-closed eyes and a distant expression, sleep-walked to the sofa, made himself comfortable, and closed his eyes—that was it.

I tried to engage contact with him in various ways. I would ask him, for example, if there was anything that he wanted to talk about that day. He would respond: "Nothing, there's nothing. Na, really nothing ... There's nothing *extraordinary* to talk about." Or I would simply wait, and after a while Mr. B. would collect himself and say: "Well, are you going to ask me anything? You are the therapist, aren't you? This is supposed to be all about me." Or I would talk about his "sleeping", and he would tell me: "It's got nothing to do with you; I've been working a lot lately."

It would not have been productive to ask Mr. B. repeatedly to think of a topic that moved him. In his mind, he could not find anything that was problematic. He was looking for an atmospheric relief in mood. He always felt well if there was someone in whose presence he was comfortable. It was only when this narcissistic harmony had been attained that he could "scan through his daily life" and talk about something.

The goal early on in therapy should be one of connecting the patient to that which really exists, thereby stepping beyond the narcissistic-oceanic feeling of well-being (Balint, 1981). At this point there is no deep discussion and the therapeutic work is not continuous.

Mr. B., for example, could never remember the content, the experiences, or the insights he gained from earlier sessions. He was not at the stage of retaining anything for himself. Everything was only alive when it was echoed by the present.

Mr. B. would often ask me: "What did we talk about the last time? I don't remember. Please tell me, you must remember what we talked about. Do you have it written down somewhere?" I would respond: "We will both try to connect to the last session and find our path. Do *you* remember anything at all, perhaps a feeling, a situation, a word or two ...?" If Mr. B. was actively involved with anything at this point, he was involved with the present, most of all with my present outer appearance. He would ask me if he should have done therapy on me that day because I looked so pale or he would remark on my lipstick and so on. With patience I would try to discover what had brought him to this topic. I would try to figure out if and why it was important to him. My impression was that Mr. B. was not even aware of his insinuating behaviour. He really had no feeling for appropriateness. At this point it would have been too early to confront him with his "inappropriateness". Mr. B. would have fallen back into his narcissistic reverence and discarded the confrontation as "unimportant", or he would behave himself and learn not to say things of this sort anymore.

b) Accepting defensive (covering) structures

Mr. C. came to therapy at a point in his life when his narcissistic self-experience had tipped to the negative side because of professional and private "failures". He had experienced a great catastrophe. He talked in a quiet and meaningful manner. He felt "deeply depressed, completely incapable of attempting anything". Further, he believed: "It is all over for me. I have my eyes wide open now. All my life I have lived a false pretense. There is no hope for me; the only option left is to commit suicide."

When I asked if he could attempt to change his situation—which from my perspective did not seem as dramatic—he answered with a mild but firm negation. His dear friends had already talked to him about the same issue. It was quite nice of them. But they could not see the entire expanse of his problem (On this matter he was right). Of course, in Mr. C.'s eyes, there was *no one* who could really see his problem in its entirety—how could they! (In this regard he was wrong).

Fortunately, Mr. C. was patient with me, his therapist. At this stage he needed the narcissistic protection of the great catastrophe. Otherwise the sadness and fear of his "wasted" life would have caught up with him. In this situation he felt strongly that his life was wasted. Remaining in the narcissistic mode, I confirmed his point of view that this was certainly a very difficult phase of his life and that it was indeed hard to change it. Yes, it was even a great, personal achievement to simply bear the situation.

Only after I narcissistically strengthened him, were we able to deal with the problematic topics. Only much later could we discuss the "tragic impersonal" life of Mr. C., in particular, the extremely destructive and annihilating way he dealt with himself. One could sense these underlying problems when we discussed earlier issues.

c) Strengthening compensational structures

Mr. A had come to the point where he wanted to move in with his girlfriend. He disregarded the opposing arguments of his girlfriend because he attributed them to her histrionic, unreliable behaviour in making decisions.

MR. A: That kind of behaviour isn't normal. *She* should be in therapy. It's like I am running up against a wall.

TH.:   In order to not always run up against a wall, it may be important to listen to these arguments and fears, to listen to your girlfriend and ask her questions. If you do this, you may be better equipped to bring about a positive change in your situation.

During this first stage, therapy is about "using the narcissistic wind for sailing". By this I mean that the therapist accepts the narcissistic grandeur of the patient. In order to expand the patient's abilities, the therapist makes use of his narcissistic ambition. With these abilities the patient may learn more appropriate relational behaviours. This enables the patient to have new experiences which can serve as an advantage and a relief in relationships. The narcissistic self can only be critiqued benevolently and *en passant*, otherwise the patient would be overwhelmed by a fear of nothingness and shame (the structure of the ego would be weakened). This, in turn, would strengthen the narcissistic, defensive attitude.

Maturity

The new experiences of the patient lead in time to structural growth (compare Längle, 2002). On the basis of these structures, therapy tries to establish contact with the immature, inexperienced "child" inside the narcissist. This is done within the safe zone of the therapeutic relationship. It is not the intent of therapy to cause "embarrassing" and shameful events for the patient who is inexperienced in social relationships. Therapy attempts to work on the weaknesses and inabilities in a natural and objective manner. General statements like, "Every person feels uncomfortable in such a situation," help in the process of therapy. They give the patient a certain amount of narcissistic protection.

The first phase of therapy uses the narcissistic ambition as a motivation for new experiences. The present phase uses the "curiosity of the child" as a motivation.

"Twilight of the gods", or, "from self-glorification to self-critique"

When the narcissist regains a relationship to himself and to others, the self expands. But he also sees more clearly the emptiness and loneliness that come with the narcissistic experience. He can also form a clearer picture of the opportunities that have slipped by and his experiences of failure. His greatness has been damaged. It is no longer beyond reach. This leads to the critical phase of therapy. The new self is not yet firm. The narcissist is shocked when he sees missed opportunities, failures, and, often, his own responsibility in these matters. The newly gained insights deepen the depression and may even lead to suicidal tendencies. The narcissist is in danger of fleeing back to the narcissistic grandeur of his earlier self. He may then notice that the facade cannot be recovered completely anymore. There is, however, the opportunity to accept and bear the "nothingness" and the depression of the present stage. The patient may grieve and leave behind the former view of himself and its air of grandeur.

MR. B.: Getting to know myself more and more is not pleasurable for me. The superior and easy role I played before is crumbling. I am not an odd character anymore; I am nothing special. I am just ... an ordinary person with nothing to say. Horribly average ... I have lost the view I had of myself. Now I have nothing left.

TH.: There is nothing left of the former character.

MR. B: Now all that is left is me—and I don't like myself.

In order to seize the opportunity of the crisis, the patient must "get on the other side of the relationship to himself"—he must leave the side of devaluation and exaltation and step on the side of empathy and attraction towards himself. He must leave behind the grandeur of self-love and love himself as a whole person.

Saying goodbye to narcissism

It is only when the patient develops a feeling of empathy for himself that he is increasingly able to leave behind his self-view of grandeur.

As Mr. B. came closer to himself, he was able to feel the pain whenever he treated himself in a merciless and repressive manner. The "reflex" of escaping to his self-view of greatness became merely a longing for it. The beginnings of his authenticity had not gained sufficient weight due to his lack of a personal history. As such, it had yet to become a compensational weight to the wishes of his imagination. The present phase was concerned with critically viewing his self-grandeur as to its significance and weight for his experience of self-worth. He was also supposed to form a clear picture of how confined he was as a result of keeping up his self-exaltation.

During therapy James Bond gave us some assistance:

Mr. B. was on the topic of movies again—he knew a lot about them. On the side, he told me: "I like James Bond movies—they're great!"

TH.:   What is it about them that you like?

MR. B: They are just shamelessly great.

TH.:   What is great about them?

MR. B: He can do everything. All the women love him. He does everything with ease and is always superior to everyone. He's got everything under control.

TH.:   He is absolutely perfect.

MR. B: He's great, untouchable. No one can threaten him or compare to him.

TH.:   That could be boring too. A person only has substance when there are imperfections.

MR. B: Hmm, interesting remark. But seriously, I would like to be like James Bond.

TH.:   What would be better then?

MR. B: I wouldn't have to be afraid of not being able to do something. The worst thing is when I want to do something but I can't, when I lose my superiority …

TH.:   In which situations would you need the assistance of James Bond?

At that point Mr. B. was starting to accept his (alleged) weaknesses. He was also learning to accept the accompanying pain of not being perfect anymore. This phase of therapy was also about taking a "critical" view of the "costs" of wishing to be a person who no one can injure or insult, a person who is absolutely great. When we took this path, Mr. B. began to approach his lack of relationships and the security that accompanied his idealised conceptions. He was then able to slowly let go of his concepts.

Further phenomenological deepening dealt with his wishes and desires: relationships, recognition, closeness, and respect. We also explored where he might have experienced or lacked these values, where he might have been hurt.

At this point in time it was appropriate to address the causes for his hidden and secretive self, to lift the pain from the depth of his life story. Mr. B.'s issues concerned the insults he had received owing to to his physical appearance, the distance to the world he experienced in his parent's home, his unhappy mother, and the many relatives who had died in the concentration camps. Mr. B.'s issues also included everything else that had not been classified a problem in the past because it had been classified as "simply the case". He was able to grieve for all of these things. In short, one could say that he was able to integrate his painful experiences.

A prognosis—realistically speaking

Kernberg (1988) wrote that narcissistic people do not believe in the necessity for change unless they are pressured to deal with it by the environment on account of their symptoms. In later years they often face a ruined life. When the power of grandeur fades, when nobody wants to hear the stories anymore, and they have become obsolete in their profession, they remain in an unreal world and complain about the evil and ungrateful world. They simply cannot admit that they have contributed to their situation or done anything wrong.

Therapeutically, the prognosis is better if the narcissistic self-view of grandeur has been unstable and if there are many affective parts to it. The prognosis looks grim if the projection and the accusations are firmly established and if they dominate the person. Kernberg makes the further observation that the therapy of narcissistic personality disorders can only be effective if there have already been a series of painful experiences. Yet, there should not be too many; otherwise the bitterness of the patient will close them off to all outer influence. Kernberg views the years from forty to the early fifties as the most opportune time for change because at this point the narcissistic satisfaction decreases (satisfaction due to outward appearance, success, etc.). This forces the narcissist towards self-realisation.

In conclusion

Citing the experiences of daily practice, it is a profitable achievement if the authentic person develops alongside the narcissistic configuration and is able to critically view the latter. In this way, the narcissistic influence is decreased. However, this step of progress often takes several years when dealing with a narcissistic personality disorder in therapy.

References

Balint, M. (1981). *Die Urformen der Liebe und die Technik der Psychoanalyse.* Frankfurt/ Berlin/Wien: Klett-Cotta.

Kernberg, O. (1988). *Innere Welt und äußere Realität.* Frankfurt/Berlin/Wien: Klett-Cotta.

Kohut, H. (1976). *Narzißmus.* Frankfurt am Main: Suhrkamp.

Längle, A. (1992). Was bewegt den Menschen? Die existentielle Motivation der Person.Vortrag 1992 in Zug, veröffentlicht in: *Existenzanalyse, 16* (1999): 18–29.

Längle, A. (2002). Die grandiose Einsamkeit. Vortrag 2002 in Salzburg, veröffentlicht in: *Existenzanalyse, 19* (2+3): 12–24.

CHAPTER TWELVE

Anna: the child wounded in her boundaries

Michaela Probst

"Don't be so hysterical! Don't act up like this! You are not the most important person in the world! I just can't handle this child anymore! She is driving me insane!" Teachers, pupils, and parents often expressed statements like these when talking about Anna.

Anna was ten years old and in the fourth grade of primary school. Her overly fashionable appearance and her capricious manner made her the centre of attention. In school she wore fashionable clothes and make-up. She had long brown hair, which was often tied in a pony-tail. Anna was slim, taller than the other pupils, and moved like a mannequin. Her appearance was vivacious, even charming, and also somewhat flirtatious. She had a radiant personality and a well-developed talent for being the centre of attention in a group.

The problematic child

Although Anna was a pretty girl, her behaviour made her unpleasant because she exaggerated everything. She was too happy, too energetic, too flirtatious, and her clothes looked like they were straight out of a fashion magazine. Her presence drew people towards her yet at the same time pushed them away. It was hard to get close to her. She kept her distance in a conversation.

Anna did not integrate herself well in social situations, although she was often the centre of attention. She could not accept boundaries or humble herself when the social setting called for it. The other pupils and teachers could not calm her down. She started a riot when boundaries were set for her. She screamed and threw punches. She locked herself in the bathroom, started crying uncontrollably, and threatened to kill herself because she just could not take it anymore. Outbursts like these often had seemingly insignificant casuses. They occurred when she did not win a game in gym class, or when she was not allowed to be first in line, or when she had the feeling that the teacher was not paying enough attention to her.

Anna had another side to her. This pretty girl, who seemed so radiant and superior, also appeared to be very fragile, lonely, and unhappy. When she was not the first at something, she began to panic and hit the people around her. She provoked other people. They misunderstood her, distanced themselves from her, and passed judgment on her.

Fortunately, her teacher regarded her behaviour as an expression of need. Despite all the difficulties, she made an effort to help Anna and did not ignore her. Anna's teacher did not want to silence her with discipline. The teacher noticed that Anna did not want to change in the changing room for gym class. In the safety of the teacher's locker room, Anna showed the teacher her back. It was covered with lines (almost like stripes) and bruises. Injuries like these occur when a child is beaten with a whip or something similar. Anna did not want to talk about how her injuries had come about. Anna was given permission to sit and watch the class and not participate. She did not have to change in the locker room. Anna made her teacher promise not to talk about her bruises to anyone.

Some time later the teacher noticed that Anna had new bruises. Her behaviour escalated more and more and she threatened to kill herself repeatedly. Anna's teacher began seeking help. The issue was finally addressed in a teachers' conference.

The beginning of therapy

Anna was obviously in need and this need could not be overlooked any longer, despite Anna's expressed wish for secrecy. A public confrontation would have disrupted Anna's trust. I was asked to help since I was a psychotherapist and a teacher who helped pupils with personal matters. I was to ask Anna if she would have a few sessions with me.

When I picked Anna up for the first time from class she was surprised. But she immediately agreed enthusiastically. I had the feeling she liked to be in this distinct role. I told Anna why our meeting had come about. I told her that her behaviour in school had worried her teacher. It worried her when she locked herself in the bathroom or threatened to kill herself because she could not handle things anymore. I told her about the teachers' conference and the decision that I speak with her. Anna was quite willing to have sessions with me on a regular basis. She came several times a week. The head teacher gave Anna permission to leave class during this time.

In one session she spontaneously said: "I have the feeling no one likes me. I don't like it when they lie to me. Everyone's taking advantage of me. I am all alone." When I asked her what she meant, Anna explained how disappointed she had been about a friend telling her she would be right back during break. But her friend then went and played with other kids. She felt deeply insulted, mistreated, lied to, and overlooked when the teacher had promised her that she could hand out the pupils' notebooks and then did not keep her promise. In moments like these, she had a deep feeling of despair. She felt lonely and abandoned. She wanted to scream and cry. She locked herself up in the bathroom so no one could see how bad she felt. When she was alone and safe, she cried and sobbed. She had the feeling of not being able to take it anymore and wanted to die. It would have been unbearable, though, if the others had seen her like this and she did not want them to. She was ashamed of her weakness and afraid of being laughed at and devalued. After Anna felt she had cried enough, she would get a hold of herself. She would then feel well enough to put on her radiant smile, open the door, and present herself to the others as the person everyone knew.

Anna and her family

It was important for Anna to keep her confession secret. She wanted to make sure no one knew how she was really doing. This included her teacher. Anna did not want her teacher to know that she was suffering out of fear that her father might find out during a consultation. Time and again, Anna made sure she could trust the confidentiality of our talks.

It was impossible for Anna to sit down during our sessions. She ran, jumped around the room, and hardly ever looked me in the eye. She seemed restless and driven, and she talked in leaps and bounds. She blocked my questions about her family. She even left the room if I stayed on this topic. She was only willing to talk about her girlfriends and daily life at school.

I hoped Anna might find painting peaceful. So I suggested she should bring her painting materials to our next session. She agreed enthusiastically. During our fifth session Anna began to paint. Without assigning a topic, she drew this picture.

At first she drew only the outer grey frame and faceless head with four legs. She said: "This is a tiny mouse that always screams." Then she added dark spikes to the back of the mouse. She described these as deep stripes. She then drew the tail of the mouse. She emphasised that the tail was wobbly. She wanted to express this by adding a jagged edge to it. In addition, she said that the tail was too big and that not everything was right with the picture. Not everything was

Anna's first picture: the balance mouse.

the way it should be. Anna then drew the inner life of the mouse. She divided it into four parts. The front part was dark purple and represented "general things". The green part was the "frightening part". The blue part was the "nothing special part". And the light purple part represented "the good". She then sprinkled the paper with light and dark dots. The light parts represented good and the dark parts represented bad.

When I asked Anna if she wanted to name the picture, she took it and placed it in front of me. She said: "This is the Balance Mouse." Before I could ask anything about the picture, she jumped up and ran out of the room. She ended our session in her typical manner.

The secret

A week later we met again. This time I suggested magically transforming her family members into animals. Anna was willing to follow my lead.

Her brother was a peaceful, friendly bunny. She often did things with him and spent much time with him. She drew her mother as a horse with large teeth. Anna thought of her mother as a biting and caustic horse. She was often angry with her and scolded her. If Anna did not obey her, she was not allowed to play outside. Her mother would lock her up in the apartment and threatened to tell grandpa about her disobedience.

She drew her father as a nice cat. Yet it was the cat that could also hiss angrily. He was rarely home because he worked on the new family house. When Anna felt bad, he was the only one to whom she could go. He understood and comforted her.

Her grandparents were represented by fish. They lived in their own apartment within the same house. Anna said: "The fish swim quickly although they are old and have many wrinkles."

She drew a dolphin to represent herself. She swam in the same water as her grandparents. It was very important to her that dolphins could swim very fast, faster than other fish. She compared their agility and speed to her own behaviour during breaks or in gym class.

Then, suddenly, Anna confessed something to me: "I have a secret. But this is no one else's business. Only I know about it. I will never tell my secret to anyone. My parents are never to know about it." On a new sheet of paper Anna drew the following picture.

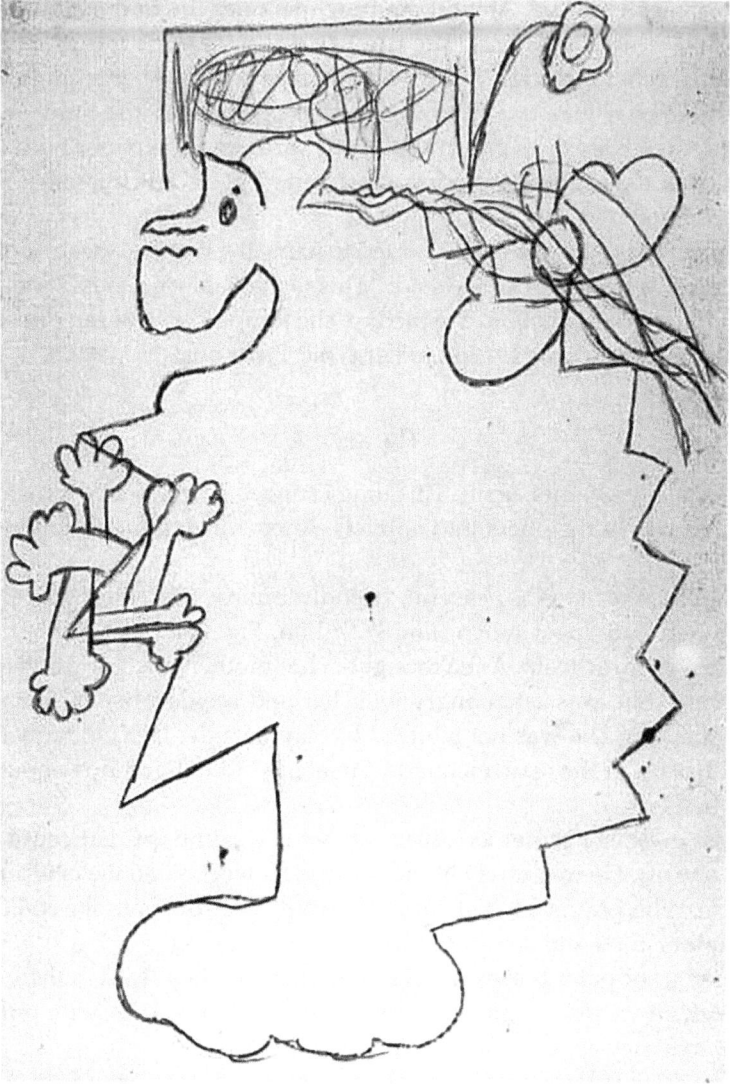

The Imagination Man.

"This is the Imagination Man," as Anna called him. She did not want to talk about him any further. But I did not want to leave Anna alone after confessing her secret. I sensed her loneliness and, in my view, this loneliness was connected to the secret. So I asked Anna about it.

I said: "I think your sadness has something to do with your secret." Although she did not reveal it to me, we established a bond that day because I knew about her secret and no one else did. Nonetheless Anna was very much alone and so I gave her my home phone number and address. I wanted to be available outside of school hours. Anna wrote the address and phone number down and kept the paper in her shoe. At home she wrote everything on the side of the door with a pencil.

The whirlwind

Before we could meet again things began to develop on their own. A parents' evening had taken place in the interim and Anna's teacher had spoken to her mother about Anna's inappropriate behaviour in school. She did not make explicit mention of the marks and signs of abuse on Anna's back but wanted to know how she was doing at home.

The mother described Anna as extremely difficult. She was overburdened by her screaming and extortion. Sometimes Anna would scream so loud that she was afraid the neighbours might call the police. Anna had repeatedly stood on the balcony on the fourth floor and threatened to jump off. She did this when she could not hold her own in a conflict with her mother or when she felt imprisoned and punished. Her mother did not know what to do and had consulted a paediatrician. The visit to the doctor, however, had not led to any results. Anna had laughed hysterically at the doctor's office and pounded the table monotonously using some sort of object. When they left the office, Anna had said: "What does that guy want from me? He is so stupid, he doesn't know anything."

The teacher was alarmed because of the suicide threats and how overburdened the mother clearly was. She demanded that the mother contact a psychotherapeutic facility for children, otherwise the school would do it for her. A couple of days later Anna had an appointment for a consultation. The teacher told me about these developments after the parents' evening.

In order to combine efforts, I called the child therapist and told her about my perceptions of the matter. I told her about the obvious signs of physical abuse, about Anna's bizarre behaviour and the suicide threats.

After a family session the therapist told me she had the strong suspicion that Anna was being sexually abused. Anna's parents had acted surprised when the therapist confronted them with her suspicion. But

shortly thereafter they were more at ease with it. They could not believe
the accusations and had no idea who the perpetrator might be. Further
appointments were made for Anna and her parents.

I had another talk with Anna shortly after this. She seemed intro-
verted, closed off, and defensive. She was hesitant to talk about the visit
to the child therapist: "That woman is so stupid. I just sat on the rocking
chair and said nothing whatsoever. I am not going there anymore. My
teacher is stupid. She told my mum to do something or she would. It is
the teacher's fault. I don't like the psychologist, I don't like the doctor,
and I don't like my teacher anymore either. She had promised not to tell
anyone. But she didn't keep her promise. I don't want to go to the psychologist anymore. I am not saying anything anymore. Not a word."

Anna began to shake. She seemed tense and confused. "Can I paint?"
she blurted out. Anna painted as if mad. She painted weird lines over
the whole page. It was a messy picture of wild jagged lines and stripes.
After this she drew cloudlike, dark shapes with two heavy yellow dots.
Anna said: "This is a whirlwind. Everything is twisting, blowing, and
it has a lot of power. The yellow dots are supposed to make everything
well again. They'll set things right."

The hurt

During the following sessions I could only get through to Anna by
exerting a lot of effort. She boxed herself in, seemed disturbed, and
often had tears in her eyes. She said: "Everything is shit. I don't want to
talk anymore or else I'm leaving." Anna closed the curtains, pounded
the keys on the piano, or threw the eraser at the blackboard. For several
sessions I merely held out with Anna. I was just there and let her throw
her tantrums.

When Anna painted, she could not depict any objects. The colours on
the page ran and mixed. She tore up her pictures and glued pieces from
one picture onto another. I tried to talk about her secret several times
but Anna evaded me and did not address the topic. In order not to
abandon Anna, I finally confronted her with what I knew. I told her that
I knew about the bruises she had shown her gym teacher. I told her
that I thought her secret had something to do with this. Quite frankly,
I told her that I knew she was being beaten and that I was fairly certain
that this occurred at home. After I had said this Anna seemed initially
paralysed.

Finally she looked at me and started to relax a little. I had the impression that Anna was relieved. She took a sheet of paper and drew this tree.

She remained silent while drawing. When she finished she gave the picture to me and said: "This is a motley tree. It is all 'whirly'."

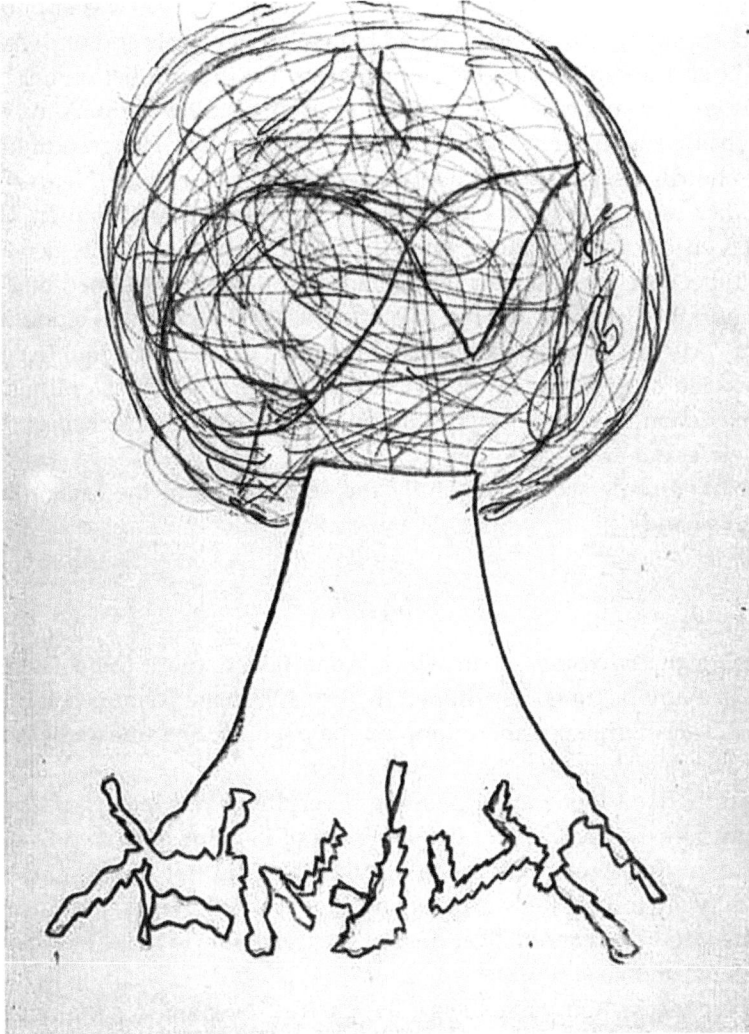

The motley tree.

During the next session Anna started to draw animals again. She started on her own accord. She drew a fish and a cat and cut them out. "The fish needs to go away. It should swim away, far away," she blurted out. "The cat has to stay though." Her grandfather should go and her father should stay with her.

Anna began to talk hesitantly. She began to talk clearly about her experiences with her grandfather. When her mother was overburdened with her, she called her father, Anna's grandfather. He was supposed to discipline Anna. Anna then had to take off her pants and underwear and her grandfather laid her on his knees. He then hit her on her bare bottom with his hand. Sometimes he used a riding whip. Anna was often alone with her grandfather when this happened. Her grandmother was hardly ever there and her mother only once or twice. Neither her mother nor her grandmother tried to restrain the grandfather. They even encouraged his discipline. They told Anna that it was her own fault because she had behaved so badly. Anna also mentioned that her grandfather had touched her in other places when she was alone with him. "My grandfather has always hurt me. I do not want him to come back. He must go far away and never come back." She literally said: "They should put my grandfather in jail. He has to be locked up and never let out again."

Now I understood more fully the significance of the Imagination Man's hands.

The relief

During the two sessions in which Anna talked about the abuse, she drew many pictures. She dipped the brush in paint, slammed it down on the sheet of paper and crumpled the page up. She smeared glue on her hands and then on the sheet of paper.

Anna liked this way of painting. Everything was sticky, dirty, and slimy. She especially liked the sliminess of it. Anna appeared to be in her own little world when she did this. She did not run around chaotically anymore. She was quiet and more settled. Her actions seemed more intentional and deliberate. She was now able to make eye contact with me and keep it up.

Five weeks had passed since the parents' evening. A social worker was contacted because of the parents' lack of cooperation with the psychologist. There were undeniable indications of physical

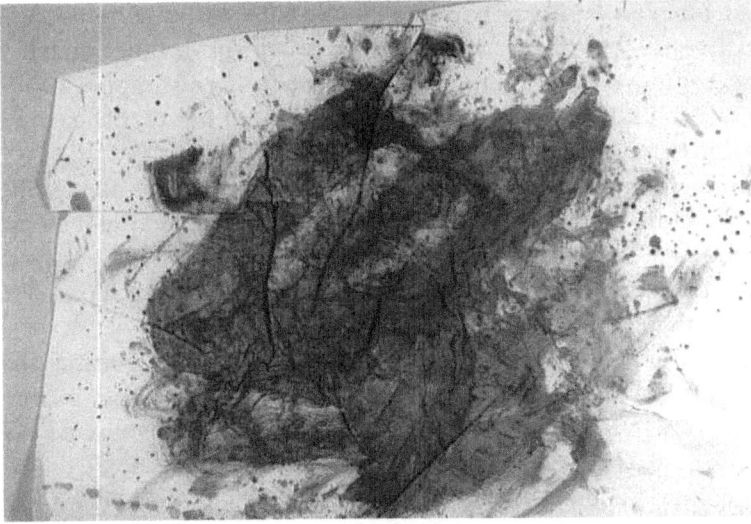

Discharge of emotions.

abuse. The social worker now visited the family several times per week.

Anna had mixed emotions about the social worker. On the one hand, her grandfather stayed away from her and the abuse stopped. On the other hand, her mother said she must be a good girl or they would send her to a home. The social worker would take her away.

The changes in her environment and the work done in our sessions had a calming effect on Anna. Her pictures became more colourful and lines appeared. There was now more structure to her paintings as well. Anna drew a picture with a narrow stripe and a big, blue spot in the middle. "The black stripes are evil," she said. "The evil has become less and the colourful stripes are the good. The blue is also evil but it is tied up now."

Protection

It was June and the school year was almost over. Anna thought about what would happen. The house her parents had built was almost finished and during the break Anna would move into the new house. In the fall she would attend a different school. Anna seemed relieved and was happy to move into her new home. She would live there with her parents. Her grown-up brother and her grandparents would remain in the apartment. It was important for Anna to remain in contact with me and I assured her that she could call me anytime.

In our penultimate session it was Anna's wish to draw with me. She took the picture of the balance mouse out of her folder and put it on the table. She suggested a game. We would take the inner life of the mouse, which consisted of the four parts, and draw a picture for each part. We would draw something in connection with each colour.

Anna started with the green part. This had been the colour that she had used to depict the "frightening part". Anna described her picture like this: "There is water everywhere. There are raindrops that do not flow anywhere. There are creepers and algae which can pull me down. At the bottom there is a rock. A tree grows outside of the water. I like everything about the tree, but I don't like the tree trunk." That was all she said about her picture.

Anna then drew the dark purple part of the mouse. This part represented "general things". Anna said: "The house has no windows on this side. All the windows are on the back side. There are also purple flowers which can only bloom in the sun." She also drew a head. She called him "the Motley". She did not like the head but it also belonged to the picture.

Finally, she worked on the light purple part, the part representing the good. Anna remarked: "The picture shows the good whirlwind which drives out all the bad people. The wind rushes by the good people but the bad people are blown to a cave. The cave is in the ocean. This is where the bad people are punished. It is only when they promise to be good that they are allowed on earth again. If they cannot keep their promise they are exiled forever." I asked Anna who would be able to create such a whirlwind. "God can do that but God cannot come down to earth. If he doesn't make a whirlwind, there are others who help him. These are lawyers, judges, and witnesses who have survived it. One can collect evidence and take the bad people to prison. A lot of people are locked up there."

Anna got up and went to the piano to play the whirlwind. The whirlwind started with high notes, it was quiet and hesitant. It grew increasingly louder and ended with low notes. Anna started to dance. She spread her arms and spun around the classroom. She said: "The wind blows and blows. It will never stop; it will keep on going forever." She seemed relieved when she walked out of the room.

During the last session Anna drew the mouse again. "This mouse is much better. Everything fits. The mouse is doing better, and it is grey. A mouse is supposed to be grey. All around her she is red because everything is ok and she is doing well." The heavy, dark stripes had disappeared. "I am also doing well now. I have become quite different in school. I don't have to lock myself up anymore. And at home I am also doing better. Next week we are moving to our new house. I am happy to go."

Anna's view of herself now corresponded with the view others had of her. In the weeks that followed Anna did not act up anymore. She stopped trying to be the centre of attention and did not lock herself up in the bathroom anymore. She no longer threatened to kill herself. Anna and I had to end our sessions because she moved away to the new house with her parents. I talked with her on the phone once more in the autumn. She readily told me she was still doing well and, indeed, her voice sounded open and credible.

The grey mouse.

Retrospection

What had happened during our sessions? What had led to Anna's improvement?

There had been changes within the family environment which protected Anna from further abuse: the presence of the social worker and the family's awareness that Anna's problems had become public. This protection had led to a rapid relief and relaxation. The new house, which physically removed her from her grandfather, also helped. External circumstances had clearly aided the psychotherapeutic work.

My talks with Anna were guided by the existential-analytic understanding of the person as Alfried Längle (1990, 1992, & 1993) described in personal existential analysis and in the existential fundamental motivations. In daily life Anna had felt rejected, even threatened by her "inability to be a certain way". She was unable to be her unique self. Whenever she drew attention to herself and her unique needs, she was misunderstood. She experienced rejection regularly and did not feel that others truly perceived her. This continuous hurt to her person was coupled with physical abuse. The beatings and the sexual abuse humiliated and devalued her. Anna had no one anymore. She did not have another person, a "you", with whom she could "become herself".

It was important in our talks for Anna to always have enough room to be herself. Anna experienced a relationship in which the other person perceived her as her unique self. This person even valued and respected her. In this atmosphere she could be herself. Within this protective zone she could develop her creativity and work through her traumata. She could then take the first steps necessary to deal with her experiences. The experience of being accepted provided a constant and dependable basis that enabled her to come close to herself.

Anna had a great creative talent. She found her own way of expressing herself. She expressed her hurts by dancing, playing the piano, and painting. Through these creative talents, she took her first steps in dealing with her experiences. She escaped the threat and fear that had silenced her. The external developments supported the process of distancing herself from her experiences.

During our sessions I supported Anna in being who she was. I sensed clearly that it was good for her to be the way she was. I understood her well in her uniqueness and could let her be. I could clearly sense how hurtful the disciplinary measures had been to Anna. She felt rejected and abandoned. When she experienced someone else bearing and respecting her in her unique way, Anna was able to stand on her own feet. She found peace within herself again.

References

Längle, A. (1990). Personale Existenzanalyse. In: A. Längle (Ed.), *Wertbegegnung: Phänomene und methodische Zugänge* (pp. 133–160). Wien: GLE-Verlag.

Längle, A. (1992). Was bewegt den Menschen? Die existentielle Motivation der Person. Referat bei Tagung der GLE am 3. April 1992 in Zug, CH. Veröffentlicht 1999 unter dem Titel: Die existentielle Motivation der Person. In: *Existenzanalyse, 16* (1999): 3, 18–29.

Längle, A. (1993). Das Ja zum Leben finden. In: A. Längle and Ch. Probst (Eds.), *Süchtig sein. Entstehung, Formen und Behandlung von Abhängigkeiten* (pp. 13–32). Wien: Facultas.

CHAPTER THIRTEEN

Sandplay: therapy with a child of divorced parents

Astrid Görtz

Introduction

Psychotherapeutic work with children requires truly perceiving them, realizing their needs and opportunities for expression. It is often hard for children to express emotions, thoughts and needs with words. Playing is a way of communicating. It allows them to reveal their inner life and express symbolic messages.

If an adult shows empathy for the "language" of a child and replies to the psychological means of expression, the child is freed from blocks. The child can then integrate severed feelings and undergo a development towards increased self-confidence, creativity of expression and courageous behaviour. This development then leads to psychological well-being. It is an amazing and truly enriching experience for the therapist to see such a change take place.

The beginnings of child psychotherapy

Sigmund Freud addressed the role of child play in 1908. He emphasised its importance: "Every playing child acts like a poet. He creates his own world. To say it more accurately: He places the things of his world into a pleasing order. It would be wrong to assume that such a child does not take this world seriously. On the contrary: He takes playing very seriously ... The opposite of playing is not seriousness but rather—reality" (Freud, 1908, p. 214).

The analyst Melanie Klein was the first to use toys in the process of treatment. She used toys in play therapy to stimulate the imagination of the child and cause associations (Klein, 1983, p. 16). Erik Erikson suggested that psychologists should recognise play as the royal road to the unconscious (cf. Erikson 1940 in Ekstein, 1994). This was obviously an alternation of Freud's statement that the dream was the *via regia*, the royal road to the unconscious.

For Donald Winnicott playing was also very important. "Especially during play and only during play [can] the child and the adult ... freely develop their creative abilities and make use of their whole personality" (Winnicott, 1973, p. 66).

Playing also provides possibilities for older, verbally advanced children (and adults) to safely, accurately, and easily express their emotions. Playing is important because language is limited. Its limitations are revealed in situations of intense emotions. For children, pictures are an essential enhancement of expression, when they are not merely taken in passively of course, as is the case with mass media. Children have only limited possibilities for verbal expression. The therapeutic setting supplies the necessary space for spontaneous and unintentional free play. It is a space where tensions, fears, and fixed conceptions can be loosened. Playing is the foundation of the entire human world of experience (cf. Winnicott, 1973). It is pivotal to the psychotherapeutic treatment of children.

The method of sandplay

The origins of sandplay go back to the analyst Margaret Lowenfeld. She explored the thoughts of children and the way they express themselves before they are able to speak. In 1929 she began to develop the "world game". She used a cupboard that was stored full of items from around the world. She used items from current movies, theatre plays, and fairy tales. The items were originally placed on a table. In further developments a metal box was used at the request of the children. The box was painted blue on the inside to portray water. It was filled halfway with sand. Water was supplied as well as shovels, forms, filling funnels, bridges, tunnels, and also plasticine, in which the children could use to make things that were not in the cupboard (cf. Lowenfeld, 1976, p. 442; cited in Rasche, 2002). "In simple words, which were appropriate to the age and the psychological maturity," Lowenfeld explained to her little patients that "most children have inexpressible ideas in their minds". She told them that "many ideas can be expressed more easily through pictures and actions than through words. This is a natural way of 'thinking'. The apparatus was then shown to the children and they were urged to play with whatever came to mind. While the child constructed their 'world', the therapist sat close by and observed the child attentively. They showed interest and helped the child in any way necessary" (Ibid., p. 243). Lowenfeld explained: "Children appropriate the things they find. They attach imaginary characteristics to them. Thereby making vehicles out of objects; they become carriers of concepts, wishes and fantasies which were created in their minds ... When they have created all the elements which they need for playing, they move on to combining these elements. These [objects] can then express all the underlying ideas which the children are trying to grasp" (Lowenfeld, 1935; cited in Rasche 2002).

Dora Kalff, a Swiss Jungian analyst, studied with Lowenfeld in 1956. Kalff used sandplay as a method of therapy for adults as well as for children (cf. Kalff, 1996). Several items were offered to the patient in therapy: a wooden box that was filled with sand and many miniature models, like puppets. These included pets, wild animals, pieces of furniture, cars, and other practical items. The box also offered the patient miniature models of objects from nature, such as stones, shells, feathers, etc. There was a seemingly unlimited variety of objects and this greatly promoted symbolic expression.

Child therapists praised the sandbox because it was so versatile. They tried not to pressure the child while choosing a medium. At first many children went for the sandbox only after they had tried other playing materials such as building kits, colours, and board games. It was often the case that essential therapeutic progress was achieved through sandplay. I suspect that it takes a certain amount of courage and confidence in the therapeutic relationship to use the unstructured material of the sandbox. At first the sandbox may even portray the image of a "boring desert" or of emptiness. Yet many children are attracted to the sand because it is a familiar material. Sandplay offers many opportunities for expression. The children may express themselves scenically as well as tactilely and kinaesthetically. It provides a method of nonverbal communication.

What "heals" during sandplay therapy?

On a basic, primary level, sand is an earthly, worldly, fundamental experience of existence. It connects us to the ground, to the foundation, and transmits security. Even seriously handicapped children can experience something immanent and eternally substantial through tactile reception. They can let the sand run through their fingers, throw it or pound on it, for example. The consistency of the sand (hard or soft, wet or dry) makes it possible for children to feel different qualities of existence. In other words, the children may transmit their own inner state onto the sand. Sand corresponds to various inner experiences and enables children to let go of inner feelings and turn towards something that exists outside of themselves. When dealing with the sand, the children turn to a protected part of the world. Sand is non-threatening, it simply exists. During sandplay, the children experience that they too can simply be. They experience a completeness and stability in their existence. This is a fundamental experience, the "ability to simply be", described in the personal fundamental motivations of Alfried Längle (cf. Längle, 1999).

These accumulated experiences lead to the experience of inner security, space, and, owing to the child's self-motivated activity, protection. The fundamental experience of simply being creates a distance from the overwhelming inner world. It is a first step in experiencing oneself as separate from the world and teaches the basics of dialogical exchange. This process is the main emphasis of phase 1.

On a secondary level, a child finds encounter and relationship in sandplay. In a sense, the sand can be "made alive" while it is formed and sculpted. This creates space for one's own liveliness. The child can sculpt mountains and valleys, lakes and rivers, waves and crevices. These "creations" can mirror a child's own "landscape of the soul", by bringing to life the things that are important and precious to her. In this creative act she encounters the things that move her. The child encounters her personal values. Experiencing her own liveliness further emancipates the child from a confrontation with burdening experiences. It promotes the state of "liking to live" (cf. Längle, 1999) within the child. This creative aspect is also used in various forms in art therapy. This is a substantial part of therapy for depressive children, for example.

The therapist should also confirm the child's expressions of liveliness. He should empathetically accompany the child. Empathy eventually makes the experience of fundamental value possible. This value essentially says, "It is good that I exist" (second personal-existential fundamental motivation, according to Längle, 1999). When working with children, playing together is the first opportunity to practice and realise empathy.

On a third level, sandplay offers multiple opportunities to children by using miniature figures and items. The children can "create scenes", act out roles, and thereby discover their own selves. They can live and be distinct. On account of this, they may recognise and value their "way of being" (third personal-existential fundamental motivation, according to Längle, 1999). Sandplay also offers the possibility of projecting experiences—especially experiences with family members—into the scenic setting of the puppets, of the figures, and of the animals. Children can reveal their abilities, their real or aspired strengths, but also their hurts or rejected and socially unacceptable feelings. It is especially important in child psychotherapy to have the possibility to express feelings, intentions, and attitudes in a "hidden" and symbolic way. This is the fundamental stylistic device in performance art. Most of the time, playing remains on a symbolic level. This serves to protect the child from a sense of shame. Otherwise it would hardly be possible for children to express traumatic or burdening experiences. By playing along, by mirroring the emotions and experiences of the figures, but also through thoughtful questions and interventions—without being overly revealing—the therapist encourages the distinctiveness of the child and the taking of a personal position. This, in turn, strengthens the self-value of the child and encourages growth.

The case study of "Anna"

Anna was an eight-year-old girl who lived with her mother after her parents' divorce. Her mother's new boyfriend also lived in the house; Anna got along with him quite well.

Anna often suffered from strong headaches and nausea that regularly followed visits to her father. This was the reason a child psychotherapist was contacted. The mother noticed that Anna—who was generally a quiet girl—hardly talked at all after visits with her father. She said almost nothing about the time spent with her father and seemed generally burdened. The mother considered making a request to change the visitation rights. But Anna was quite attached to her father and he would certainly have fought for his rights.

When I first met Anna, I noticed that she was very serious for her age. She did not readily reveal her inner life. Yet she was quite willing to take part in the games and project tests being offered (the scene-test and completing the beginnings of sentences, for example). Anna discovered the fascination with sandplay in the sessions that followed. During these sessions, she depicted various family scenes with the aid of the puppets. She created the following scene: the mother was lying in the deck chair and beside her was the crib with a baby. Close by, two other children were playing in the sand. Grandma and grandpa were also nearby. Opposite the deck chair was a crocodile. The family was fine though as the crocodile had eaten and was full.

In a phenomenological, descriptive way, one could say that the picture depicted a diffuse threat to the idyllic family scene. Yet the threat was not urgent. During the talk that followed, Anna explained that she would like it very much if her parents got back together again.

The "threat" of the crocodile could have to do with the breaking-up of the family. Anna's mother had told her about the divorce. Anna told me that she felt pressure in her stomach when she thought about this. Anna then reached for the hand puppets: the princess and the crocodile. The crocodile woke up the princess. It chewed on her skirt and her hair. Punch then came onto the scene. The crocodile bit into his hat but lost several teeth in the process. Although it now had only a few teeth, the crocodile bit off the nose and the hat of Punch. It also bit off the nose and the braided hair of the Gretel-figure. It bit off the hair and the robe of Hansel. The grandma also lost her hair. "Now everyone is done for," Anna said. The only one who was still present was a second Punch figure. It hit the crocodile.

I later found out that aggressive and emotional scenes had preceded Anna's parents getting a divorce. The mother said she had been hit by her husband. He, on the other hand, said that she had threatened to throw herself out the window. He had had to violently prevent her from doing this. Anna had witnessed this scene.

During an extensive talk with Anna's father, I realised that he was a very sensitive, differentiated, but at the same time strongly depressive person. His world had collapsed on account of the divorce. Anna's father

Scene of family with crocodile.

was born and raised in the former Yugoslavia. His ideal conception of a family was of a large family clan, the way his family was at home. On account of this, the divorce was a personal tragedy. He seemed quite bitter. He complained about the overall state of society and was not open to any offer of help. On the contrary, he thought it shameful that his daughter needed therapy. Anna seemed to be the only person he was close to. In her he confided his depressively tainted thoughts. He did this in order to instil "proper" values into her. He did not realise that he was burdening and overextending her.

After speaking with the father, it was not surprising that Anna was depressed herself. The psychosomatic symptoms were clear expressions of her inner tension, a tension caused by the pressure her parents placed upon her.

The first step of therapy was to convince both parents to cooperate with each other. This would be in the best interest of their daughter. Yet this attempt failed because of the bitterness on both sides. At a minimum, therapy was supposed to offer a neutral place for Anna, a place where others understood her difficult situation, a place where she could find her own emotions. Therapy consisted of therapeutic play methods as well as the story "The Search for Rainbow Tears", written by Jorgos Canackis. This is a story that deals thematically with divorce and the death of one of the parents. The story made it easier for Anna to find space for grieving.

I want to now turn to some sand pictures and sand scenes. They illustrate Anna's development within therapy. The development can be divided into five phases. The interpretations and insights have been put in italics because they were made after a considerable time gap.

Phase 1: A threat to an idyllic family scene

As we saw in the previous picture, Anna at first depicted various family scenes. These expressed an idyllic harmony. Increasingly, animals were depicted in the scenes (goose, monkey, stork). Yet they also displayed a threatening aspect, a threat to the peace and harmony. In one scene, for example, the stork bites a little girl's face without any warning.

Like all children of divorced parents, Anna held on to the conception of an "idyllic family". It was a central theme for her. In my view, the father promoted this feeling because he also held on to an ideal conception of family, a conception of an "intact family clan". He could not let go of it and therefore could not grieve.

Scene of family with a baby.

Phase 2: Scenic aggression between the figures

Anna discovered a new way of sandplay: she buried approximately ten puppets in the sand; two other puppets looked for the buried ones. They stomped on the buried ones while looking for them. These figures called out in pain: "Ouch, ouch." This scene was a contrast to the pictures of phase 1. In these, the threat had come from outside the family, from animals. But now the puppets had turned against each other. Anna openly enjoyed expressing her aggressions in this form.

These scenes point to Anna's way of dealing with her experiences. Her experience included the suffering of "powerless" victims.

Another variant expression of this motif was the sandstorm: sand blew in the face of the figures; it rained down on them from above until they were completely buried under it. Some of them turned into mummies; the grandfather became the pharaoh. We were in Egypt now. The sandstorm blew away the deck chair and everything else. Only a hand of the pharaoh-mummy stuck out of the sand. The children discovered his hand at some point in the morning and were very scared. They dug out the mummy and, fortunately, it was still alive.

Anna dramatically emphasised her comments about these scenes. She said: "Now something horrible is going to happen again!" or, "Now everyone is lying in a heap again. They are a family of course, so why not?"

At this point Anna was playing quite mirthfully with the border between life and death. In this way Anna was able to live out the scary threat of the aggressive scenes between her parents, especially her fear for her mother (as mentioned earlier, the mother had threatened to throw herself out of the window). But she could also relive her own fears during this time and thereby, as it turned out, overcome them to some degree.

Quite interestingly, a reoccurring motif was the threat to a child. This threat was also present during the sandstorm phase: a baby was carried off by the waves of sand and buried beneath it.

Phase 3: direct sculpting of the sand, playful interaction with the therapist

During these scenes it was my job as a therapist to verbalise the events of the scenes and to mirror the emotions of the figures. I did this without interfering with the scenic actions. The level of the play now changed. The scenes changed from a mere scenic approach to a dialogical sculpting of the playing material. Anna adapted the burying scenes and made them closer to reality. Now it wasn't the puppet that had to search for the buried figures, but I, the therapist, who had to search for them with my eyes shut. Anna tried to make it increasingly hard for me.

In this phase Anna also wanted to incorporate and sculpt the sand more intensely as a formable material. This step could be foreseen by the rain of sand during the sandstorm. Now we also used water and the sand was moist. This made it possible to sculpt the sand into towers, mountains, and tunnels.

Anna began to ascend out of a complete immersion in the inner world of her imagination. She began to spontaneously sculpt the sand. This demonstrated self-trust and trust in our relationship. She did not seem to be cornered anymore, but appeared to be more free and strong. She was now able to approach reality again.

Anna really enjoyed playing in the sand. When therapy began, she had wanted to wash her hands immediately after playing. Now she enjoyed digging in the "mud" and "caking" her hands with the wet sand. Eventually, she no longer used the figures, only a great deal of sand and water.

I had clearly noticed that Anna's mother had a strong disciplinary influence on her. Both of them, mother and daughter, were always dressed fashionably and proper. Anna always behaved very "well" when her mother was around. All this made it harder for her to deal with "negative" emotions like anger, rage, and aggression. During this phase Anna lost her shyness and overcame taboos, like "getting yourself dirty", for example. Anna was joyfully engaged in her own liveliness and had perhaps overcome her depression to some degree.

Phase 4: discovery of creativity: anna as an architect of her own home

After the intensive "mud" experiments, Anna returned to her scenic play. Again, she depicted family scenes. But now it was not the figures that were the centre of attention. Now she sculpted a place to live, a home for the family.

Anna showed herself to be an artistic architect. She sculpted caves and houses which were several stories high! She patiently supplied these houses with furniture. Every family member was taken care of; everyone had his or her own room. The baby, especially, had a protected place for the crib. Anna assigned the role of assistant to me. The assistant was supposed to supply water and sand. During this phase Anna said that she would like to play in the sand every day.

Anna's houses were in fact quite lively. Scenes from everyday life took place inside. There was a little dog that jumped around the house; it was quite chaotic at times. In contrast to the houses of the first phase, these new ones were equipped with a bathroom and a toilet. This was done quite early in the construction phase. Anna enjoyed the "toilet scenes". One family member after the other had to wait outside the door in order to use the bathroom.

Anna discovered her creative talent. I was astonished by her ability to work with the soft sand. Anna enjoyed her newfound liveliness. In fact, she enjoyed the everyday, close-to-life situations particularly because these were taboo at home.

It appeared that Anna distanced herself from the early family pictures. She now constructed a lively home for herself in her imagination. On the one hand, this enabled her to overcome her mother's need for order. On the other hand, Anna was able to free herself from the pressure of her father. Her new pictures

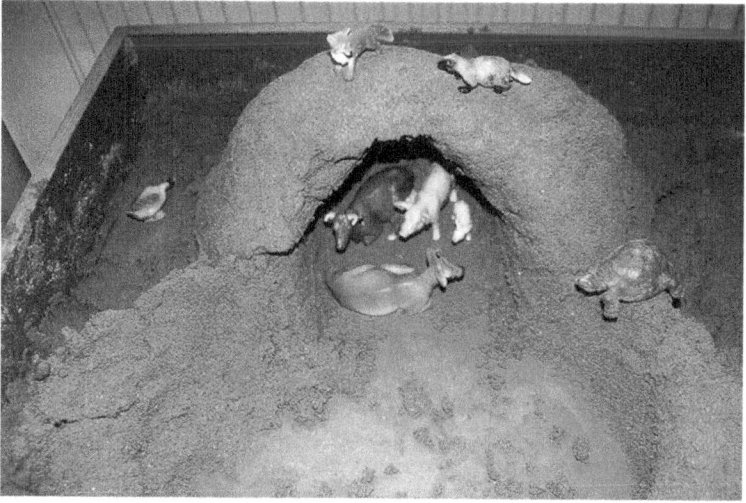

Barn.

Multistorey barn.

might have been quite similar to her grandmother's life in Yugoslavia, but these pictures were truly her own. Anna was always enthusiastic about all of the animals on her grandmother's acreage. It was perhaps this ideal that the father had carried inside of him. Anna could now enjoy this ideal without feeling

obligated to her father. This step of "emancipation" could be seen later on when Anna started to criticise her father. In therapy it was possible to openly talk about the issues with her father. We talked about the fact that her father was not doing well and that he urgently needed help. During these talks Anna was no longer burdened but relieved. She let go of the responsibility for her father and handed his well-being over to adults. After a while Anna refused to visit her father periodically.

During this phase of therapy Anna wanted to show her mother, for the first time, what she had done in the sessions. Until then she had rarely spoken to her about what went on during therapy.

Anna now felt strong enough to stand her ground in her relationship with her mother. She took the first step out of a childish assimilation towards adopting a personal position. At this point she still needed the therapist to back her up.

Phase 5: development of inner distance, overcoming the separation of good and evil

Anna not only sculpted houses but other things as well. She made landscapes with hills and imaginative constructions like a "mountain of stairs" with a glassy throne at the top, mysterious swords, two mysterious but "not so costly" glasses, a mysterious key, etc. The mountain of stairs had treasures inside "which belong to the king. Whoever touches them has to do a certain task." There was a snake which swam in the water around the mountain. Mum and Dad were going on a walk. The snake scared both of them. Without paying attention to this detail, Anna jumped right to the end of the story: "Now they have mastered all the dangers!" The king said: "You may have all the treasures, including all the water and the animals." Mum and Dad were allowed to sit on the throne. The fear of hidden dangers kept coming back. This time it appeared in the form of a fairy tale, which had a typical happy ending. Yet the path to this happy ending was not quite clear to Anna at this point.

She now used figures of princes and knights. There was good and evil, yet no clear distinction between the two. One could generally say that her distinctions between "good and evil" seemed very artificial. Anna commented on the scenes in a very resolute way, which was almost ironic: "The sun blinds our eyes, so we'll darken everything because the evil people like darkness." About a guard she said (speaking hyperbolically): "Well, look at that guy (he is unshaved), a typically evil guy!" Now the dragon came into play: "The dragon is on a mission. He has to fight the evil people; actually he has to fight the good people!" Two panthers also belonged to the evil side, even though they looked quite nice. The queen went on walks and maintained order. "She isn't quite sure if she really wants to be evil. She says to the owl to get the sword because she wants to fight against her husband because he is evil ... At some point the land becomes the land of nice people; whoever gets the key can decide if the land is supposed to be evil or good." In the meantime, the dragon had become nice, and the panther too—he was licking the queen.

At the end of the session Anna showed her mother the scene she had created. Her mother grew silent and seemed taken back.

Anna's stories had become more cryptic and symbolic. They mirrored her struggle to find her own position. Did Anna wish to possess the key? Did she expect therapy to be the "key" for her? The animals and fairy tale creatures turned from evil to good. With humans that might not be so simple. But judging from Anna's comments, and especially by her tone of voice (which is difficult to reproduce here), one noticed that she could not take the adults' distinction between good and evil too seriously anymore. She gained inner distance towards her parents' relationship. From her perspective, the world was no longer straightforward and simple, but had undergone a change.

Children of divorced parents live—just like other children too, only much more so—in two separate worlds: in the world of one parent certain things are good which are bad in the world of the other parent. This throws children into deep inner conflict. In Anna's case, the relentless fight between mother and father for the "right" values was intensified by the cultural background. Even for adults, it is often not easy to discover the relativity of their morals. For an eight-year-old child this is even more the case.

In concluding this case study, I believe the sand pictures described have shown the possibilities for children to deal with extremely difficult and traumatic divorces. They may overcome their situation by creatively expressing themselves and through the accompaniment of the therapist. One also notices that child psychotherapy is limited to a certain degree, especially when it comes to working with the parents. But Anna's story also reveals children's own resources and abilities, namely, their abilities for "self-distancing" and "self-transcending" (for terms cf. Frankl, 1984). On this basis, they are able to take a personal position towards things, including their parents. Supporting children in their adult environment is an obvious part of child psychotherapy.

The role of the child psychotherapist

The therapeutic process, as it developed in the case of Anna, demanded a very specific type of therapeutic attitude. As an existential analyst I would call this a "phenomenological attitude". This attitude includes an understanding openness and not the opposite, interpretative explanation. Working with children calls for an emotional expression of "childlike openness". It is about sensing what is important to the child at that moment without adding or over-"looking" something. It is hard to formulate this type of perception in words because it includes an "all-encompassing impression" of the mood and atmosphere of the therapy session. Quite often, therapeutic, theoretical interpretations can only be drawn in retrospect. During the session, however, events remain in a state of childlike emotionality. Even when the therapist becomes aware of interpretations and explanations, it is not appropriate to take a superior view and verbalise it. Changing to an explanatory position would evoke a sense of shame in the child, and in the worst case scenario it would traumatise the child all over again. This is certainly a decisive difference to working with adults, although even with adults an "interpretation" can often be quite inappropriate and should instead give way to "non-verbal understanding". Attaining this attitude demands practice and experience. One has to get to know (get in touch with) one's own ideas, judgments and interpretations in order to leave them aside in therapeutic work. For the child therapist, that which is best (simple or even naive) is the result of hard work.

During the first phase of Anna's therapy, I confined myself to the role of a "witness". I wrote the scenes down in detail yet I also explained to Anna beforehand what I was doing "because it was important for me to memorise what she was building". Otherwise I was simply verbalising what went on during the scenes. I "mirrored" the emotions of the figures or asked questions when I was uncertain about something. I asked questions like: "Grandma and Grandpa are lying on the deck chairs. Are they just resting?" Or I said: "The crocodile is sitting close by." Anna then naturally explained in detail what went on during the scenes. In this way she came to experience her emotions more clearly. She became more secure in how she felt emotions and gained self-confidence. This made it possible for Anna to express direct, aggressive emotions, as happened in phase one and two.

The therapist takes on a different role when a child calls for a direct interaction with the therapist. After phase three, my role increasingly changed to that of a playing partner. I let the child decide which role I should play and attempted to keep to the prescribed "rules of play". These did not have to be explicitly expressed. Most of the time children articulate their demands non-verbally. At this point it is up to my "sense" and "intuition" as therapist to not "fall out of the role", to not overstep boundaries, and, on the other hand, to not become passive and frustrate the child's desire for a shared experience. At the same time, this means that the therapist cannot follow his own interests in play but must adopt a certain role that supports and promotes the child. Here, as well, the phenomenological attitude, sensing what the child wants at the moment, what they need, and what is good for them, is of utmost importance. All this depends upon the degree of activity of the therapist.

A concluding remark on interpretations: they are of course quite important to the progress of psychotherapy. Understanding the total situation is important for determining in which direction therapy should go, if I should advise the child to talk with their parents, if the school should be contacted, etc. Such an understanding develops from a pool of knowledge and experience but—and this is the main point— also from an evaluation of how the child is experiencing the situation at the moment.

Working with the parents

I have mentioned several times that the accompanying work with parents and other important relations (teachers, house parents, grandparents) is an essential part of child psychotherapy. Even if the personal resources of the child are strengthened through individual work (which may in fact have a long-term effect on the child), the fact that children are extremely dependant on adult authorities cannot be overlooked. If the energies (which influence the child) within the environment are not taken into consideration, therapy could easily worsen the conflict within the child's soul instead of improving it.

In Anna's case, such a conflict was already underway because of the differing value systems of the parents. Therapy is not supposed to promote these conflicts. At the beginning of therapy it was important to realise what kind of feelings Anna had towards each parent. In regard to her father, she seemed to give off the impression of wanting to "save" him. As a therapist it was my duty to take part of that responsibility off her shoulders. Addressing the issue of a psychologically ill parent is a great relief for children. Therapists experience this constantly. When I offered to speak with her father myself, Anna was able to let go of her sense of responsibility to some degree. I made the first appointment with the father after a few sessions with Anna. I had asked Anna for her approval beforehand. After a few months we had another talk in which the father said that he was not willing to accept help from anyone. At this point in time Anna had already let go of this conflict to some degree and was hardly troubled by it anymore. In my view, this change in attitude came about because of the individual work done with her.

During my work with the mother I tried to dismantle the controlling influence which she had over her daughter. This influence also extended itself to therapy. For the first session the mother had given Anna something of an order. The mother knew what her demands were for therapy and which topics should be discussed with her daughter. She imagined I would talk about Anna's father—which to a certain degree was in fact the case—in order to convince her that he was in the wrong.

When divorced parents try to bring their relationship conflicts into therapy, the therapist needs to make sure that they offer a "neutral place" for the child. The child must be allowed to feel her emotions without getting into trouble with one of the parents. This also involves not addressing the critical aspects of the child's relationships to her parents. The child loves her parents and is also dependent upon them. It is important for the therapist to accept the parents of the child without passing judgment on them and respecting the deep solidarity of the child–parent relationship. This basic principle is essential, even in the case of abusive parents (The issue of "child protection", which may conflict with this principle, cannot be addressed here).

The child therapist works within a field of tension. He must convey to the parents that the child needs the freedom of the sessions in order to get well psychologically. But at the same time, the therapist must not jeopardise their willingness for cooperation. I had to tell Anna's mother, in a friendly but firm manner, that we had to have a clear setting for therapy. She had not been handling things very well (appointments were cancelled, sessions were irregular, etc.). I also had to remind her again and again that what went on during a session was confidential (by law). Anna needed firm protection during this phase. She had not talked to her mother about anything that went on during sessions. To prohibit an increase in the mother's pressure on Anna, I invited her to talk with me. I told her about the progress Anna was making from my point of view yet concealed the content of the sessions from her. I confirmed her decision to seek therapeutic help for Anna. Because of these conversations, Anna's mother felt that she was being taken seriously; it also strengthened her in her motherly role. It was especially important for me that she not perceive therapy as a "competing rival". This would soon have resulted in a cessation of therapy. Things became quite difficult when we talked about Anna's father. She tried to make me take her side in the matter. She could not see her own role in the relationship conflict clearly. The first time I offered to have a talk with the father, she was suspicious of me. I had to make it clear to her that I was completely on Anna's side. I was merely interested in strengthening her and that I would not get involved in the relational problems of the parents. After my talk with the father, I clearly noticed the unsolved problems in the relationship. At this point I had to confine myself to some degree. I was quite tempted to address the relationship problems, but I had to realise that neither of them was willing to understand the situation of the other. The reciprocal hurt had left deep wounds. Working with this issue would have also extended the boundaries of child psychotherapy.

Anna's mother had child custody, so she was the one I worked with. Like the mother, the father had also doubted the meaningfulness of Anna's therapy. He did not take me up on my offer for another talk after a few months of therapy. I did not have any more contact with him after this.

Instead, Anna's mother wanted to visit me after a year. She wanted to bring her new partner as well. I then met Anna's stepfather. He appeared to be an understanding man who was concerned for Anna's well-being. It was my impression that Anna's mother was doing better with him at her side. She felt more secure. This also had a positive effect on her relationship with Anna. Anna accepted this man more and more as her "new" father.

Nevertheless, I believe it was important for Anna's development that an attempt was made to bring the parents closer together again. Even I, the therapist, had not managed to do so. If this could be done, Anna could let go of her sense of responsibility for her parents.

During my last talk with Anna, after she had visited her father in Yugoslavia, she told me that it had been "boring". She was very excited about a skiing vacation with her mother, her stepfather, and another family who had a daughter her age. The distance to her father was now growing wider and wider. This is a common development after a divorce takes place. It is most certainly difficult for the separated parent. But, in Anna's case, it was evident that the father missed his opportunity by not being willing to confront his own pain. It saddens me that there are few cases where a child maintains a relationship with both parents. Often divorce means the loss of contact between the child and one of the parents.

References

Ekstein, R. (1994). Die Bedeutung des Spiels in der Kinderpsychotherapie. In: G. Biermann (Ed.), *Kinderpsychotherapie: Handbuch zu Theorie und Praxis*. Frankfurt: Fischer, [1. Auflage 1976 bei Ernst Reinhardt: München].

Erikson, E. H. (1940). Studies in the interpretation of play: I: Clinical observation of play disruption in young children. *Genetic Psychological Monographs, 22*: 557.

Frankl, V. (1984). *Der leidende Mensch: Anthropologische Grundlagen der Psychotherapie.* Bern: Huber.

Freud, S. (1908). Der Dichter und das Phantasieren. *Gesammelte Werke*, Bd. 7. Frankfurt: Fischer, 1965.

Kalff, D. M. (1996). *Sandspiel: Seine therapeutische Wirkung auf die Psyche.* München: Ernst Reinhardt.

Klein, M. (1983). *Das Seelenleben des Kleinkindes und andere Beiträge zur Psychoanalyse.* Stuttgart: Klett-Cotta, 4°.

Längle, A. (1999). Existenzanalyse—die Zustimmung zum Leben finden. *Fundamenta Psychiatrica, 12*: 139–146.

Lowenfeld, M. (1935). *Play in Childhood* [republished New York: John Wiley & Sons, 1967].

Lowenfeld, M. (1976). Die „Welt"technik in der Kindertherapie. In: G. Biermann (Ed.) *Handbuch der Kinderpsychotherapie III* (pp. 442–451).

Rasche, J. (2002). Das therapeutische Sandspiel in Diagnostik und Psychotherapie. Stuttgart: Opus Magnum. Available at: www.opus-magnum. de/rasche-joerg.html (accessed November 2015).

Winnicott, D. W. (1973). *Vom Spiel zur Kreativität.* Stuttgart: Klett-Cotta.

CHAPTER FOURTEEN

Encountering a disabled person: attitude and experience of the therapist

Karl Rühl

When we encounter a disabled person, we are reminded of our own wounds and limitations. In this sense, a disabled person challenges the therapist and therapy can prove to be quite difficult. When we look at this issue in depth, we realise that the therapist and the patient often have similar feelings during the therapeutic process. A question arises: who is really the patient here? It takes courage and humility to descend from our position of superiority. Humility is the foundation of the therapeutic attitude and the foundation of the existential-analytic approach.

I would like to illustrate this theme using the case study of a woman with multiple acquired disabilities. I would also like to use the case study of my most difficult patient, namely, myself.

On the anamnesis

I encountered Mrs. Meier while I was doing home care work. She had a recurring malignant tumour in her brain. Her disabilities were the result of the operations performed on her brain, which had made her more and more disabled. She was confined to a wheelchair. Her face and vocal cords were paralysed. She had lost her sense of smell and taste, and she was growing increasingly deaf. Mrs. Meier had been an attractive, happily married mother of one. Her family ties soon broke because of these massive changes. Her husband and child had left her.

On existential analysis

Mrs. Meier's personal integrity had been challenged; she had even lost it to some degree. She could not integrate her disability. She experienced herself as bound to her disability. This experience and attitude created a further self-inflicted disability. Because of this, she had lost almost all reference to the world and to herself. More and more she failed to reach out to her own values. Since she could not reach her values, her lifestyle was more oriented towards loss and not towards fulfilment of values. She devalued her abilities and strengthened her destructive tendencies through passivity.

On the therapeutic attitude

When we encounter a disabled person, we are also forced to confront a concealed issue in life: the question of existence. The therapist derives his self-understanding and an understanding of his work from the position he takes towards this question of existence. The word *therapeuo* originally meant "being close to someone by serving them". The meaning later became "reconstituting" or "healing". It cannot be the goal of therapy to rid the patient of her disability. The goal of therapy should be to reconstitute her original wholeness and unity. This is the result of being close to someone by serving her needs.

The person who works with the disabilities of other people is called to confront his own weaknesses and disabilities through self-experience. The therapist needs to "cultivate his own weakness". If the therapist, in spite of all the applied empathy and valuing towards the patient, remains a "giant" to the patient, he will not be able to accept his own unique weaknesses during the therapeutic relationship. When the therapist has confronted his weaknesses, he can serve and help the other person to accept her personal weaknesses.

Viktor Frankl wrote: "The Self becomes a Self only by contacting a You" (Frankl, 1983, p. 13)—he makes a reference to Martin Buber and his dialogical principle). The meaning contained in Frankl's statement can easily be twisted. It could mean that the underdeveloped self of the patient becomes a self when in contact with the therapist. This is not the case, however. The self becomes a self in connection with a "you", within a reciprocal exchange of giving and letting others give to you. It is not only the patient who is being healed. The therapist receives treatment as well. This does not imply that we have to or even should disregard traditional therapeutic roles, but this is how I understand Frankl's call to rehumanise psychotherapy.

How to practise this therapeutic understanding

Each disabled person lives in a unique world of personal experience and therefore requires specific forms of treatment. Yet there is a common undertone or thread in the treatment of disabled persons: the question of how they deal with their circumstances, with the pressure, their particular disability, with the suffering that ensues, and the unique position they take towards their own world. Depending upon the person's behaviour, she can either afflict herself with another disability or create strengthening power. Existential analysis has an approach and attitude that is quite unspecific. According to Längle (cf. Längle, 1992, pp. 361ff.) it is the goal of "unspecific existential analysis" to:

- stop the client from wallowing in passivity and the escalation of the negative;
- stop the negation of her circumstances, which means being able to incorporate present conditions into living circumstances;
- create a realistic and new orientation for the patient, especially for people who have suffered irrevocable tragedies.

Stopping the flood of passivity and the escalation of negativity

When a disability is not integrated, the self becomes overwhelmed and a person loses reference to the world. The self becomes alienated from the person. The person then destroys her desires and abilities and subsequently suffers from loneliness.

This escalation also occurs because the person tries to protect herself from further hurt. In the case of Mrs. Meier, this self-protection became all-encompassing and led her to avoid both the world and the self. As a consequence, she was engulfed in passivity, which manifested itself in self-destructive tendencies. It was my primary aim, therefore, to provide relief for Mrs. Meier. In order to do this I needed to perceive *myself* accurately so Mrs. Meier would not have to suffer the opinion of a helpless stranger. It was not appropriate at this time to take therapeutic action, but rather to draw myself back. I had to do this so Mrs. Meier's own movements could be recognised, respected, and valued again.

Disabled people, as well as non-disabled people, have strengths and weaknesses. It is the therapist's job to uphold the strengths in order to enable the patient to develop these abilities further. The stronger abilities have to be integrated. Many people approach disabled people with the aim of helping them deal with their disability and with themselves. But this kind of help is often pathological at its core. We overlook the fact that underneath these statements is an attempt to progress beyond the disability, to connect to certain values, or to distance oneself from the disability. In my experience, this kind of approach is not fully addressed in therapy and therapists themselves often overlook their own adoption of it. This was the case for my patient as well. She had already developed strategies for everyday life. It was my goal to help open her further to her own abilities.

Our therapy sessions took place in her apartment. We exchanged roles. I sat down in her wheelchair and she explained to me how to get to the bathroom or from the couch to the wheelchair, for example. This helped me, to some degree, to see life from her perspective. It also helped her to break free from the imprisonment of her situation when she was able to realise her own abilities.

I asked Mrs. Meier how she was doing. She typed into her typewriter: "I feel like shit. I wish I was dead!" I felt cornered. My first impulse was to say: "This cannot be." I pushed my feelings aside because I was afraid of losing my bearings in this situation. I had the impulse to talk. Many helpful tips came to mind. But I did not proceed on this path because I felt this would dehumanise her. She would become a person with whom I could not empathise and this would push her further into isolation. I had another impulse which often comes to me when I am confronted with such hopeless cases: "If everything is truly this bad, then she simply cannot do it. She cannot live like this and should be somewhere where others take more responsibility for her." But this reaction would have prioritised my own unpleasant feelings. I would have implicitly told Mrs. Meier how incapable she was. I convinced myself that it was her right to describe her life the way she wanted and needed to. I gave her the space to complain and, indeed, she continuously complained and reviled her situation. This was accompanied by destructive tendencies and desperate gestures. She had lost her hold, and it became my goal to find some security and hold for her. In the beginning I offered her my perspective on things by being understanding and emphatically emotional. I explicitly told her how empathetic I was. The fact that someone else perceived her made it possible for her to see herself. The space I gave her made it possible for her to perceive her own space. Yet she only felt this space momentarily and diffusely, she could not accept it as a given in her life.

During this time it was important for Mrs. Meier to build a relationship to her feelings. Having the space to complain enabled her to slowly connect to values. In order to make this connection one must lift the primary emotions and salvage the buried values. The process of lifting occurs through a dialogue with the emotions, emotions that have not been fully understood. Lifting requires getting under the emotions, under the client's movements. This is done in order to supply a gentle security for the movements of the client, which do not have a firm foundation.

I asked Mrs. Meier how she felt during this process of complaining. She waved me off in resignation! She pounded on her typewriter: "I am totally exhausted. I am done for." Then she started to sob terribly and covered her face. Even though I welcomed her reaction as a therapist, it also startled and frightened me. A struggle with the conditions of her life followed. I was helpless to change these conditions. I was now concerned with both my ability and powerlessness to change the conditions of her life.

Logotherapy has its origins in Socratics. It does not view powerlessness as pathology. Powerlessness is in fact the precondition to finding a meaningful path. If I, as a therapist, can not feel helplessness, emptiness, or that I am lacking in knowledge, I am apt to approach the client with objectivity. I am then positioned above the client and can cause experiences of failure within the client. The therapeutic objective with Mrs. Meier was in fact the experience of powerlessness. It constantly led me back to my primary view of the situation. I felt a fear of desperation time and again and Mrs. Meier was right in protecting herself from this fear.

Getting to know the facts

The second step in unspecific existential analysis, namely, the process of pulling the facts in, had begun. We could proceed to this step because Mrs. Meier was able to open herself up to the reality of her life and begin a relationship to it. After the lifting of primary emotions I tried to salvage the lost, concealed, and waiting values. We began with distancing procedures in an attempt to sense valuable things. This was the time to address her methods of self-protection. Her fear was alive; yet it was not necessarily a fear grounded in experience. She had a hard time with her fear because she was unable to control her inner and outer conditions on account of her disability. She therefore readily embraced temporary solutions. She tried, for example, to fight her fears instead of using them. This only increased her fearful emotions. When she attempted to ward off her fear—or deny it—by retreating inwards or compensating through aggression, she experienced only temporary relief. Yet her fear also increased after the temporary relief had passed.

My starting point was confronting the concealment of her face. This behaviour was connected to her fears and to concealed and lost values. Her concealment was symptomatic for her. She constantly looked herself over, trying to see if everything was still all right, yet refused to go out in public.

From an unspecific point of view, a symptom has a personal identity. Within a person there is a driving and enforcing power or pathos of life (cf. Kühn, 1988). For a person who is engulfed in painful symptoms, this power tries to forge a path and connect to values.

"Syn" lies at the root of the word symptom. Much like symbol, synergy, and synthesis, "syn" refers to something that belongs together in order to reach a specific fulfilment. "Ptome" expresses the complete process of a fall, a burying, and a loss. Yet the meaning of our drive for fulfilment has been misinterpreted. The fact that Mrs. Meier covered her face said a lot about her loss and about what she was protecting. We therefore began a relationship with a symptom and spoke through it. "Do you understand why you must hide your face?" Answer: "I just cannot stand it if someone sees me cry." She had often seen herself cry in the mirror. And she could not bear to see herself this way. Again, I was caught in a whirlwind of emotions. What should I say in response to this? Should I say something calming, put on a show for her ...? I could never change the disfigured face in front of me, and I could not imagine myself living this way. She asked me if I would like to have her face, what if the tables were turned. I knew what she was getting at. She wanted to know if I could live with a face like hers. Her question stunned me. I was helpless and silent. I knew I had to reverse the question, since we were in a therapy session. I asked her if she thought I would be able to live with her face. Now we were both silent. She stammered: "It is so difficult ..." "What is so difficult? To lose your face?" We talked about experiencing such a loss. She asked me what I thought about her face. Her question was somewhat inhumane, objectifying. I tried to avoid giving an inhumane reply. I asked her if we could sit down in front of the mirror together and tell each other what we saw in the other person. She agreed and explained to me which scar came from which operation, why her one eye was crooked, and so on.

Many of our talks occurred in this fashion. We did not talk about the facts directly but used alternate routes. We used a value to talk about her disability. When we worked together and parallel to each other, she was able to perceive herself and separate the distinct parts: the loss, the remaining abilities, the possibility for new abilities. Which fear was a justified fear, which fear was the result of insecurity and grief about the loss? What was the defensive mechanism that drove the fear to panic? Where could she help herself and where did she need help from others? Where was she justified in fighting for her position? Where did she deceive herself? How much space did she have and where did she give herself too much or too little space?

The new orientation

A realistic, new orientation can best be discovered if the client begins to practise new or old values. Mrs. Meier had reserved the driving service for disabled people, including the personnel, two to three times per week. She felt the strength to follow through with what she wanted to do and felt the lust for life again, but often expected too much. For example, she felt rejected after being driven to the shopping centre, as nobody talked to her. Furthermore, she was exhausted and felt powerless from going out three times a week. A new, realistic orientation simply meant that we constantly addressed the present conditions and dealt with the situation realistically.

Mrs. Meier was aware of her situation, but she had started on her path. We established these first contacts together. I was challenged beyond my comfort level. A community needs just as much therapy as a disabled person, but if the therapist works within the community, a necessary strengthening of therapy takes place. A community that is capable of integration is necessary for the reconstitution of personal integrity. At this point it is the therapist's duty to be aware of his part. It is up to him to integrate the individual therapeutic work into a communal network. The therapist may be shocked to discover that he must help the patient find such a community.

Every new activity Mrs. Meier engaged in was connected to diffuse states of anxiety. These could be efficiently handled by dereflexion (cf. Frankl, 1982, pp. 198, 253). Mrs. Meier also had a concrete fear. She was afraid that the tumour would continue to grow; she was afraid of going back to the hospital; she was afraid of having to be admitted to a home; and she was afraid of dying in "misery". I was unable to alleviate this tragedy of existence for her. Personal existential analysis is about coming to a beginning in one's life. The person can find strength in this beginning and oppose death until it finally arrives. They then have to give themselves over to death by shaping the way they want to suffer it. But a human question of existence has not yet been answered. It is the question of "existence-until-death". It is the question of the final meaning of one's life. Where does the light come from, how can I grow towards it? Which messages are hidden for me in the singularity and uniqueness of my existence until death? The prayer and meditation of Dietrich Bonhoeffer (Bethge, 1985, p. 381) was helpful for Mrs. Meier:

> Who am I? They mock me, these lonely questions of mine.
> Whoever I am, Thou knowest. O God I am Thine!

In conclusion

Hitler's personal doctor Brandt visited Bethel to convince its leader, Pastor Bodelschwingh, of the usage of euthanasia. While they were taking a walk he saw a mentally handicapped old man. Brandt asked Bodelschwingh: "Would it not be more merciful if this old crippled man, whom they are feeding precious, valuable milk, would die. We could take the milk and give it to young children." Bodelschwingh supposedly turned around and said: "This man is the most important man in my business. No other man has provided so much opportunity, for others and me, to learn how to love."

I want to say conclusively that my most difficult case, namely myself, advanced in love by encountering this disabled woman, Mrs. Meier. Realistically, therapy is more of a communal growing experience than an experience of success. If one takes this view, the differences between the disabled person and the treating therapist are not a threat but a gift. The weakness receives its strength.

References

Bonhoeffer, D. (1985). Wer bin ich? In: Bethge (Ed.), *Widerstand und Ergebung*. München: Kaiser Verlag.

Frankl, V. E. (1982). *Ärztliche Seelsorge*. Vienna: Verlag Franz Deuticke.

Frankl, V. E. (1983). *Ärztliche Seelsorge*. Frankfurt: Fischer Verlag.

Kühn, R. (1988). Arbeiten am Schmerz. In: C. P. Thieder (Ed.), *Reinhold Schneider* (pp. 77f). Wuppertal: Brockhaus Verlag.

Längle, A. (1992). Existenzanalyse und Logotherapie. In: A. Pritz and H. Petzold (Eds.), *Der Krankheitsbegriff in der modernen Psychotherapie* (pp. 355–369). Paderborn: Jungfermann Verlag.

Living beginnings

Alfried Längle

> *It matters more in life*
> *to begin something*
> *than to complete it.*

What you cannot begin in some way, remains lifeless. Without beginning, there is no life.

> I cannot grasp what you are telling me if it does not bring me to
> a beginning.
> I cannot catch what life throws at me if it does not bring me to
> a beginning.
> I even lose myself if I do not know what to do with myself.

To bring myself to a beginning: to insert my life into the world anew, like a thread into a needle.

Beginnings weave life into the world.

To always come to a beginning because it leads to simplicity, to the origin, to the source, to the new.

To always remain a child, a searcher, to rediscover out of the sense of helplessness the wideness and variety of life. To begin even if there is no guarantee I will arrive the end. To begin nonetheless in spite of everything. Because I am alive.

> Until death to be at the beginning
> Until death to be connected to the beginning
> Not being forced to master, but being able to be present

> To experience: I am capable.
> The Primary Ability!

Reproduced from: Längle, A. (2002). *Sinnspuren: Dem Leben antworten*. St. Pölten: NP-Verlag, pp. 11–12.

USEFUL WEBSITES

Institutes and Societies of the GLE

The international society for logotherapy and existential analysis, Gesellschaft für Logotherapie und Existenzanalyse—International (GLE-Int.) is the umbrella society for the international activities of exis tential analysis, with its headquarters in Vienna. Existential analysis as psychotherapy, counselling, and coaching in the form described in this book was developed by the GLE-Int., and is exclusively taught in the GLE-Int. and its institutes and national societies. The training is uniformly regulated for all countries in the world where it is taught.

GLE-International

Eduard Sueß Gasse 10
1150 Wien
Austria
Tel and Fax: ++43 - 1 - 985 95 66
E-Mail: gle@existenzanalyse.org
Web:
English: www.existential-analysis.org
German: www.existenzanalyse.org

The GLE-Int. is the largest association of existential psychotherapy worldwide, with approximately 1,500 members in German speaking countries today.

The GLE-Int. has national societies in Austria, Germany, Switzerland, Czech Republic, Slovak Republic, Romania, Poland, Russia, Lithuania, Argentina, Chile, Mexico, and Canada.

Twice a year the GLE-Int. publishes the journal *EXISTENZANALYSE*, which includes German and English articles on the theory and practice of existential analysis. For more information see the German and English webpage: www.existenzanalyse.net

Websites

Societies	
GLE-International	www.existenzanalyse.org
GLE-Österreich (Austria)	www.gle.at
GLE-Deutschland (Germany)	www.gle-d.de
IGEAP-Schweiz (Switzerland)	www.existenzanalyse.ch
SLEA-Czech Republic	www.slea.cz
SLEA-Slovakia	www.slea.sk
GLE-Poland	www.analiza-egzystencjalna.pl
GLE-Russia	www.ieapp.ru
GLE-Argentina	www.gle-argentina.com.ar
EA-Canada	www.existentialanalysis.ca
SCAE-Chile	www.analisisexistencial.cl
GLE-Mexico	www.analisisexistencial.org
Institutes	
ICAE Institut for EA in Santiago de Chile	www.icae.cl
USA	www.centerforexistentialanalysis.org

HSE Moskau (Psychology Deptartment, Higher School of Economics) http://psy.hse.ru/psychotherapy.

German speaking institutes are listed at www.existenzanalyse.org.

INDEX

195